Devotions for Girls

Ages 2-5

God and Me 3

by Lynn Klammer

I dedicate this book to all my parents. To Ron & Shirley Ittner—for the care and influence that helped to make me who I am today. For Ken & Helen Klammer—whose love and acceptance into their family has nourished and enriched my life in immeasurable ways.

GOD AND ME! 3 FOR AGES 2-5
©2012 by Legacy Press, third printing
ISBN 10: 1-58411-091-0
ISBN 13: 978-1-58411-091-0
Legacy reorder #LP46834
JUVENILE NONFICTION / Religion / Devotion & Prayer

Legacy Press
P.O. Box 261129
San Diego, CA 92196
www.LegacyPressKids.com

MIX
Paper from
responsible sources
FSC
www.fsc.org
FSC™ C013572

Cover and Interior Illustrator: Dave Carleson

Unless otherwise noted, Scriptures are from the *Holy Bible: New International Version* (North American Edition), copyright ©1973, 1978, 1984 by the International Bible Society. Used by permission of Zondervan Bible Publishers.

Printed in South Korea

Table of Contents

Table of Contents

Table of Contents

Introduction

As I write this introduction, I'm finishing this third volume of the *God and Me!* books. It's been wonderful to witness the success of these books, and to receive the lovely comments readers have sent me over the years. My four children have changed a great deal since the first book was released. However, they still continue to amuse and amaze me with their antics, and bless me with the timeless wisdom their experiences impart.

Each true story in *God and Me! Volume 3* includes a matching Bible verse, questions, and a prayer. Every devotion is based upon a theme. The activities following the devotions are designed to match the interests and abilities of girls ages 2-5 and are accomplished using common household materials.

I hope you enjoy your time with this book, as you share its lessons with that special little girl in your life. Our Lord's Word is clear in everything we do, even in everyday moments like those depicted within these pages. May His loving guidance be with you now and always.

Here are the steps to use God and Me! 3:

1. Read the devotion title and the purpose.

2. Read the Bible verse. Look it up in your Bible. Draw a line under the words in your Bible to help you quickly find the verse later. God doesn't mind if you draw a neat line in His words.

3. Read the story or have your parents read it to you. Answer the questions.

4. Think about the answers to the questions. Pray to God. Talk to Him about what you have learned. Try to spend a minute or more just listening for God's voice in your heart and mind.

5. Read the activity directions and do the activity. The projects and puzzles will help you act on what you learn.

Use this book each day in a special time alone with God.

Take time to talk to God in prayer as you go through this book. Have fun loving God and learning about Him every day!

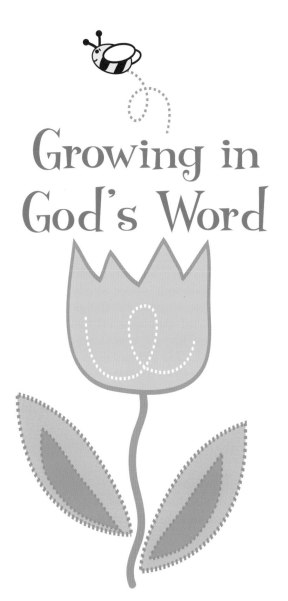

Growing in God's Word

Growing Up

Growing up is a good thing.
Your faith is growing more and more.

~ 2 Thessalonians 1:3

"You're Forgetting My Childhood!"

"Do you want your bottle?" Mommy asked little Shelly.

"Baa," Shelly insisted. "I want baa, not bottle."

"That's what I said," answered Mommy, confused by how upset Shelly was getting.

"No!" screamed Shelly. "I call it baa. You have to call it baa!"

"Why are you getting so upset?" Mommy asked.

"You're forgetting my childhood!" yelled Shelly.

Sometimes it can be hard to let go of the things you're used to. Even though Shelly was a big girl and could say the word "bottle" just like adults do, she didn't want to. It made her feel like she was losing something important. Shelly needed to know she could be a big girl and do so many things!

As you grow up, Jesus wants you to learn and to set aside the things of your childhood. It's a part of His plan for you. You will always have your memories of things you did when you were little, but Jesus also wants you to look to the future as you grow up.

Your Turn

1. What did Shelly call her bottle?
2. Why didn't Shelly want to change what she called her bottle?
3. Can you remember something that you used to like, but don't like now that you're growing up?

Prayer

Jesus, please help me to feel good about growing up, even when it means giving up some of the things I used to like to do. Amen.

Shelly's Garden

Growing up can be hard. It's easier to give up little girl things if you remember that Jesus will give you new things to do as you grow.

Here is something else that changes as it grows—a garden! Shelly loves to garden with her daddy. Look at the garden below and answer the questions.

Your Turn

1. How many leafy, green cabbages are there?
2. Can you count the orange carrots?
3. Are there more small flowers or more big flowers?
4. How many red pepper plants are there?

Names

There can be many names for the same thing or person.

If we had forgotten the name of our God...
would not God have discovered it?

~ Psalm 44:20-21

Spider or Pider?

"That's not right, Chloe," said Amy. "You're not saying the 's' sound."

Amy's little sister was pointing to a picture of a spider and saying "pider." She was leaving the "s" off on purpose.

"Mommy and Daddy like me to say 'pider' instead of 'spider,'" said Chloe. "They say it sounds cute."

"That doesn't matter," answered Amy. "It's still not right. It's not a 'pider.'"

Chloe thought about what Amy said, but she still kept saying "pider." She liked how it sounded, and it was her own very special way to say the word.

It doesn't always matter what something is called. It's still the same thing, no matter what its name is. In a similar way, there are many good names we can use for Jesus that are given to us in the Bible. There is more than one name for Him, but just like with Chloe's "pider," the name we use doesn't change who He is.

Your Turn

1. What was Chloe's name for a spider?
2. Why did Amy want Chloe to stop saying "pider"?
3. Do you have any special names for things?

_____

_____

_____

_____

Prayer

Jesus, thank You for still being who You are and that we can call you Father, God, Holy Spirit, and lots of other names You give us in the Bible! Amen.

Spinning Top

A name doesn't change what something is—Jesus is still Jesus whether you call him God or Father or another name the Bible gives us for Him.

Here's something that you can call by many different names: a spinning top, flying wheel, or maybe even a rotating disk. Whatever you call it, however, it's still fun!

What you need:

1. Cardboard
2. Safety scissors (make sure you ask a grown-up before using scissors!)
3. Pencil
4. Crayons/glitter

What to do:

Cut a circle out of the cardboard. The circle should be about four inches in diameter. Decorate the circle any way you like. Next, poke a hole in the center and insert a sharpened pencil through it. The circle should stop just above where the pencil is sharpened. Now, hold up the cardboard and pencil top, pointed side down, and spin it on a flat surface. Watch it go!

Abilities

**You must wait until you know how to do something
before you do it.**

Show me the way I should go.

~ Psalm 143:8

The ATM

"I wanna do it! I wanna do it!" cried Annie and Dave as Mommy pulled the van up to the ATM. This was the machine at the bank where Mommy put in money or took money out. It was very exciting and the kids wanted to be the ones to push the buttons, feed the envelopes into the slot, and take the money as it came out. But Mommy wouldn't let them.

"I have to do it," she said. "It has to be done just right, or it won't work." What Mommy said made sense; it was a grown up job.

Later, they went to the department store and rode on the elevator. Mommy let Annie and Dave push the buttons for the right floor. It was a job just for them!

Sometimes only certain people should do certain things—like when you're in church and the pastor does the sermon or gives communion. He's been taught how to do those things and knows how to do them the right way. Only Mommy knew how to use the ATM the right way.

Jesus wants you to do only those things you truly know how to do. That way you won't get hurt or hurt someone else.

Your Turn

1. What did the children want to do?
2. Why did Mommy say they couldn't use the ATM?
3. Can you think of something you'd like to do, but can't yet?

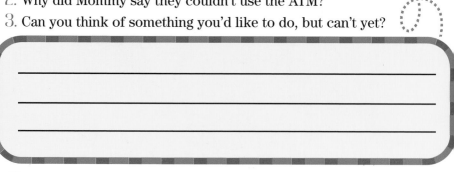

Prayer

Jesus, please help me to wait until I know how to do things before I try to do them. Amen.

Steely Figures

Jesus wants you to do the things you know how to do, and to learn the things you don't yet understand.

Here's something that may take time to understand, but if you follow the directions, you'll be an expert in no time at all.

What you need:

1. Steel wool pads
2. Cardboard or a thin cutting board
3. Safety scissors
4. Magnet

What to do:

Cut the steel wool into pieces. Place your steel wool pieces on top of a piece of cardboard. You can also use a cutting board, depending on its thickness. Slide your magnet back and forth under the board to form various designs out of your steel wool.

*Note: Parents, you might want your kids to wear gloves for this activity, as the small steel wool fibers can easily get stuck in delicate skin.

Follow Through

You should always follow through on the things you start.

Never be lacking in zeal.
~ Romans 12:11

Amber's Mess

"If you don't like to work, then why do you make such a mess?" Mommy asked Amber one sunny afternoon. Amber had been complaining about having to pick up her toys. She and her brother and sisters had toys scattered all over the house. When it came time to clean up, they didn't want to. "Why don't you kids pick up the mess since you're the ones who made it?"

"Because we want to play," Amber replied.

"Well, a part of playing is cleaning up when you're done," said Mommy.

Amber thought a moment about what Mommy was saying, and then said, "We like to play, but it's too much work to clean."

Some things just naturally go together, like playing and cleaning up. Amber didn't want to clean up. She just wanted to do the fun part of playing, but not the rest.

Jesus wants you to do all the things you're supposed to do, not just the fun parts. If you make a mess, then you need to clean it up. Always finish what you start.

Your Turn

1. What did Amber do that caused a mess?
2. Why didn't Amber want to clean up?
3. Are there things that you started but still need to finish?

Prayer

Jesus, please help me to remember to always finish what I start, even when it isn't fun. Amen.

What Am I?

Jesus wants you to finish what you start. If you finish reading the rhymes below, you'll be able to guess what the rhyme is describing. Hint: Look in the box!

I creep, I crawl
I climb on walls
I'm red, but black
Is what spots my back.

I crouch in the grass
Until you've passed
And then I spring
To hop and sing
I'm shiny and green
With antennas
That quiver
I'll live in your lawn
And sing until dawn

Details

You should pay attention to details.
Everyone who does what is right has been born of him.
~ 1 John 2:29

Little Details

"I'm ready," said Jessica, as she skipped into the room. "Look at my dress. Isn't it pretty?" Jessica was getting ready to go on a fun family trip and she wanted to look her best. She had put on her big sister's dress because she thought it was so pretty, but the dress was a little too big for her.

As Mommy looked at Jessica in the fancy dress, she noticed that it looked a little odd in the back by Jessica's neck. "Turn around, Jessica," Mommy said.

Jessica turned around and her Mommy found a clothes hanger in the back of her dress! Jessica had put the dress on all by herself, but had forgotten to take the hanger out!

Life is full of little details. They may seem small, but even little things can make a big difference sometimes. Jessica didn't think that it mattered if the dress was the right size or if the hanger was still in the dress. But it did matter.

Jesus wants you to pay attention to the little details in life. Things like holding an adult's hand when crossing the street or never talking to strangers can be very important things to remember. Jesus wants you to be safe and happy, so paying attention to details is a very good thing.

Your Turn

1. Whose dress did Jessica put on?
2. What did Jessica forget to do when she put on the dress?
3. Can you think of details in your life that are important? Are there some that aren't as important?

Prayer

Jesus, please help me to pay attention to the little details in my life. Amen.

Picking out the Details

Jesus wants you to be aware of all the details in life. By paying attention to details, you'll be safer and learn more.

Take a close look at the picture and try to pick out the little details listed below.

Try to Find:

1. Buttons that look like flowers
2. A flower in the girl's hair
3. A pocket on her dress

The Lord's Supper

We should understand the Lord's Supper and be respectful of it.

I am going to celebrate the Passover with my disciples.

~ Matthew 26:18

"Do I Get To Eat God?"

Maya loved to ride in the car with her brother and sisters after being picked up from school. There was always so much excitement as they shared the day's events.

One day they talked about the Lord's Supper. Maya had seen it on Sundays when everyone went up to the front of the church to drink from a cup and eat a small piece of bread. It was a part of church, but she didn't know what it meant. As she listened to her brother and sisters talk about it, she became concerned about when she would someday do it. The more she thought about it, the more she began to think it was funny. Turning toward her mommy she asked, "Will I get to eat God, too?"

Maya's mommy explained to her that eating the bread and drinking the juice at church was a way to remember that Jesus died for us. It was something very special and not to be joked about.

Jesus gave us the Lord's Supper as a special way to remember Him.

Your Turn

1. How did Maya hear about the Lord's Supper?
2. What did Maya ask her mommy about the Lord's Supper?
3. Do you understand what the Lord's Supper is? Ask someone to tell you about it.

_____

_____

_____

Prayer

Jesus, thank You for Your beautiful gift of the Lord's Supper. Help me to always remember that it's a serious and wonderful thing. Amen.

Ice Cream Clown

Maya learned about the Lord's Supper, and she can think about its special meaning.

Jesus likes it when you learn about new things. Here's something you can learn to do that's fun and you can even eat it when you're finished! You will need some ice cream, sugar cones, licorice ropes, and a bag of mini marshmallows.

Once you have all the ingredients, make a nice round scoop of ice cream and set it on a plate. Use the mini marshmallows to give the scoop eyes and a nose. Add the licorice rope to make a lovely smile. Top the scoop off with one of the sugar cones for a silly clown hat.

Patterns

Jesus has given you the ability to pattern your own life.

Make every effort to add to your faith…self-control.

~ 2 Peter 1:5-6

The Human Carrot

"What is Paige doing?" wondered Mommy as she watched her little girl sitting at the kitchen table. Paige had been sitting at the table for a long time, with only a small carrot to nibble on. Mommy couldn't understand why it was taking Paige so long to eat it.

After a while, Paige walked out into the living room to show Daddy her carrot. It had been scraped away in the middle, like someone had carved it out. "How did you do that?" asked Daddy. Paige just pulled her lips back from her teeth and smiled her biggest smile as she pointed to the gap where she had lost her baby teeth. By placing the carrot between the missing teeth, and then turning it, she had carved the carrot away in the center only.

Paige used her special ability to make a pattern in her carrot, just like each of us are given skills to make patterns in our lives. You can make the very best patterns in your life by following what Jesus teaches you in the Bible.

Your Turn

1. Why was Paige sitting at the kitchen table for so long?
2. How did Paige make the pattern on her carrot?
3. What are some special skills you have that you can use to make your life the way God wants it to be?

Prayer

Jesus, thank You for giving me special skills so that I can make good patterns and good choices in my life. Amen.

Special Skills

Use your special abilities to make patterns in your own life. You are special and only you can do certain, special things. As you read in the story, Paige had a special skill. There's a picture of it below. Color the picture, and think about some things that only you can do.

The Unknown

You don't need to be afraid of what you don't know.

Do not let your hearts be troubled.

~ John 14:27

What's Going to Happen?

It was Bailey's first day of Sunday School at her church, and she was scared! She just didn't know exactly what to expect, and that made her feel afraid.

As Mommy pulled up to the church and her sisters jumped out of the van, Bailey started to cry. When Mommy pointed out the teacher walking by, Bailey yelled, "That's the short lady I don't like!" and cried even harder.

"What's it going to be like?" she wailed. "What's going to happen?" The tears ran down Bailey's reddened cheeks as Mommy explained what would happen inside and that Jesus would be with her. When Bailey heard what everything would be like in the classroom, her tears began to dry. Knowing what to expect made her fear go away.

Jesus doesn't want you to be afraid. That's one of the reasons he gave you people like your parents to take care of you. When you're scared about something new, just ask someone to tell you what to expect and it won't seem so scary anymore.

Your Turn

1. What was Bailey going to be doing for the first time?
2. Why was Bailey so scared?
3. Can you remember a time when you were scared about trying something new?

Prayer

Jesus, thank You for giving me parents to tell me about new things. Amen.

Jesus' Symbol of Love

Jesus wants you to know that whenever you're scared you can always turn to Him for comfort. The cross below is a symbol of Jesus and His love for you. As you color it, think about how much Jesus loves you.

Breaking Rules

Sometimes it's OK to break the rules.

Your word is a...light for my path.

~ Psalm 119:105

Telling Private Stories?

Danielle told her friends at church how her mommy was naughty when her mommy was little. Danielle loved telling the stories she had heard her mom tell, but then wondered if she should be telling them. Her family had a rule that some things were only meant to be talked about within the family.

When Danielle told her mommy what she did, Mommy asked why she told the stories. Danielle said it was because she wanted to teach the kids how even though Mommy had gotten into trouble sometimes when she was little, Mommy always admitted when she'd done something wrong. Mommy thought about it a moment, and then told Danielle that since she was telling the stories for a good reason, it was OK.

Sometimes it's OK to break the rules if you have a good reason. Try to ask someone's permission first if you're not sure. Jesus wants you to do the right thing and help other people, even if the right thing is sometimes against the rules.

Your Turn

1. What did Danielle tell the other children?
2. Why did Danielle tell the stories?
3. Can you think of a time when you did something that was against the rules, but for a good reason? Talk to Mommy or Daddy about that time and why it was OK.

Prayer

Jesus, please help me to always do the right thing. Amen.

When to Break the Rules

Sometimes it's OK to break the rules, but Jesus only wants you to do so if it's for a very good reason.

Below is a picture of a time when it might be hard to know if you should break the rules. Look at the picture, and then discuss with your Mommy or Daddy what you would do in this situation.

Frustration

You don't need to be frustrated when you can't do something.
Do not be discouraged.
~ Joshua 1:9

What's Half?

Savannah loved pancakes, but Mommy was too busy to make her some, so Savannah decided to try making them herself. With the help of her brother and sister, Savannah looked at the pancake recipe.

"This recipe is for too many pancakes," her big brother Ethan said. "You should just make half this much."

Savannah gathered the things she needed to make her recipe, and Ethan told her what type of measuring cups she needed. Savannah got upset, "I can't do this," she yelled. "I don't know how much is half!"

Savannah was frustrated by not being able to figure out what half of each recipe ingredient was. She was still too little to make the recipe by herself.

Jesus doesn't expect you to be able to do everything you want to do yet. He knows you're still little. If you get frustrated sometimes like Savannah did, try to remember that Jesus understands.

Your Turn

1. What did Savannah want to eat?
2. What did Savannah's brother tell her she needed to do with the recipe?
3. Can you name some things that you're still too little to do?

_____

_____

_____

Prayer

Jesus, please help me to not get upset when I can't do all the things I want to do. Amen.

Bunny Cake

Jesus understands that you'll feel frustrated sometimes, and that's OK. Here's an activity that might be a bit frustrating at first, but ask your parents for help and you can do it! Before you can begin, though, you will need to get a box of cake mix, frosting, and some different candies to decorate your cake (rope licorice, gumdrops, etc.). You also need to have two 9-inch round cake pans. An adult will know where these are.

Mix the cake batter according to the directions on the box, then divide the batter between the two pans and bake until done. When the cakes have

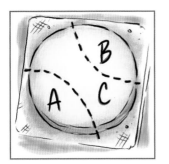

cooled, transfer one to a round platter—this will become the bunny's face. Transfer the second cake to a cutting board and have a grown-up use a knife to cut it into the shapes shown below (if you freeze the cake first it will cut more easily). Assemble the pieces of the cake around the "face" to give your bunny ears and a bowtie. Finally, frost the cake and decorate your bunny with the candy; rope licorice makes wonderful whiskers and gumdrops are good for the nose and eyes. Invite some friends over to enjoy the cake!

Not Alive

Jesus didn't give objects feelings.
Only living things have feelings.

Apply your heart to what I teach.

~ Proverbs 22:17

I Don't Like You, Door!

"Ow!" Grace cried as a loud "bang" sounded through the house. She had just run into the side of the bathroom door. It was something that happened to her quite often in that room. For some reason, that door seemed to always be in her way. She would catch the side of it as she passed through the doorway, and the door's edge would bump into her side.

Mommy heard the loud bang, and Grace crying "ow." She saw Grace looking at the door with an angry expression on her face as Grace hollered, "I don't like you, door!"

Grace blamed the door for hurting her, when in reality it was her walking into the door that caused her pain. It was silly to think that the door would understand when she told it she didn't like it. The door wasn't a living thing!

Jesus made living things and non-living things. Non-living things, like Grace's door, don't have feelings. Only living things do, like animals and people.

Your Turn

1. What happened to Grace when she went into the bathroom?
2. What did Grace tell the door?
3. Is there something in your house that you don't like?

Prayer

Jesus, please help me to remember that non-living things don't have thoughts and feelings like I do. Amen.

Living or Non-Living?

Jesus made both living and non-living things in our world. Below are some pictures of both. Can you tell the difference? Circle the pictures that are of living things.

Making Sense

You can learn from the world around you.

Pay attention and gain understanding.

~ Proverbs 4:1

Splashing Horse Flies

Alyssa and her sisters loved to swim in their pool. Alyssa usually couldn't wait to jump in, but later in the summer, there was a problem. When Alyssa went swimming with her sisters in late summer, they were usually visited by large flies. Daddy called them "horse flies" because they were so big.

When the horse flies came, Alyssa and her sisters would swat at them to shoo them away, and even splash water on them. They thought that they could kill the flies if they got water on them, but it didn't seem to work. The flies would just buzz away for a moment and then fly right back again.

Alyssa was wrong about how to get rid of the flies. Even though she could see she was wrong, she still believed she was right.

Jesus made you very smart, so that when you see how things are, you can learn. Jesus wants you to pay attention to the world around you, and learn from it, not just believe things for no reason.

Your Turn

1. What did Alyssa like to do with her sisters?
2. What was bothering Alyssa and her sisters when they were in the pool?
3. Why should Alyssa have known that flies couldn't be killed just by splashing them?

Prayer

Jesus, please help me to always learn from the world around me. Amen.

Marshmallow People

Jesus wants you to be smart. Paying attention to the world around you will help you to see things for what they really are.

Here's an activity where you can learn something new. Make sure you have a grown-up to help you.

What you need:

1. Large marshmallows
2. Small marshmallows
3. One large toothpick
4. Four regular-sized toothpicks
5. Decorating gel

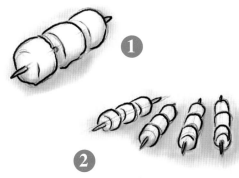

What to do:

Put three large marshmallows in a row by pushing the large toothpick through the centers (diagram 1). Push three mini marshmallows onto each of the smaller toothpicks (diagram 2). Then attach the four smaller toothpicks to the marshmallows on the large toothpick to make the arms and legs of your marshmallow person (diagram 3). You can leave the legs off if you'd like your marshmallow person to be more stable. Use the decorating gel—or anything else you wish—to give your marshmallow person a happy face.

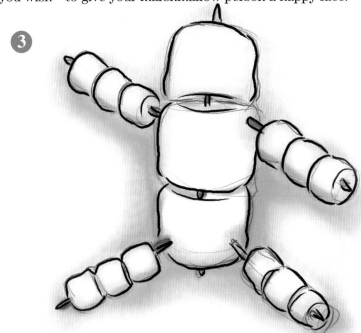

Tricky Behavior

You should never trick people.
Each of you must put off falsehood and speak truthfully to his neighbor.
~ Ephesians 4:25

Sort-Of Sick

Emily didn't want to stay at preschool today. She would much rather be at home playing. Mommy would never say that it was OK to leave school without a good reason.

Emily thought about it. If she was sick she could go home! Emily acted like she didn't feel as good as she usually did. Emily said she was sick, and soon her Mommy was there to get her.

Emily was so happy when she got home, but Mommy stopped her from going up to her room. "There are too many distractions up there," Mommy said. "Bring your sleeping bag downstairs and you can make a little nest to sleep in right beside me while I work at the computer."

Emily did a naughty thing when she tricked her Mommy into thinking she was sick and needed to go home. She couldn't play with her toys like she thought she could.

Mommies and daddies want to trust their children and when you trick them, it doesn't help them to trust you.

Your Turn

1. Why did Emily want to go home?
2. How was Emily's misleading her mommy just as bad as lying?
3. Can you think of another example of someone being misleading?

Prayer
Jesus, please help me to always be honest and never mislead people. Amen.

Matching Toys

Being tricky isn't what Jesus would want you to do. Jesus wants you to be honest. If you pay close attention to little details, you can sometimes tell if someone is tricking you. Pay attention to the activity below, and you'll find the answers.

Jenna, Beth and Katie each have a favorite toy. Can you guess whose toy is whose? There are clues to tell you which toy goes to which little girl, so look closely. If you think you know the answer, draw a line connecting each girl with her favorite toy.

Measurements

Jesus is the same, no matter how you measure his love.
But you remain the same.
~ Hebrews 1:12

How Do You Measure Jesus?

"Why are they telling us how high forty feet is?" said Daddy one morning as he watched the news on TV. "Everyone knows how high forty feet is. Forty feet is forty feet."

"No it isn't," answered Kayla. "Forty feet can be different for different people."

"How is that?" asked Daddy.

"Everyone's foot is a different size," answered Kayla. "There are lots of different feet!"

There are lots of different types of measurements. There are measurements like "feet" and "inches," and then there are other ways to measure, like when you "measure" how you feel about someone with your thoughts or opinions. What you think of others and how you feel are things that can change from time to time.

No matter what type of measurement you're using, you should remember that Jesus' love for you, and what He teaches you through the Bible, are always the same. You can't measure Him with things like "feet" and "inches." His love is always the same, no matter how you measure Him.

Your Turn

1. What was the measurement that Daddy thought everyone knew?
2. Why did Kayla say that a "foot" was different for each person?
3. Can you measure Jesus' love?

_____

_____

_____

Prayer

Jesus, thank You for love that isn't changing. Amen.

Paper Tree

Some things are too big to be measured with a ruler—like Jesus' love for us.

Below is an activity that is small enough to measure. Just follow the directions and you'll soon have something fun to play with.

What you need:

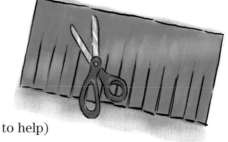

1. Paper towel tube
2. Ruler
3. Green construction paper
4. Glitter and crayons
5. Tape
6. Safety scissors (ask an adult to help)

What to do:

Have a grown-up help you with the ruler! Cut the construction paper into three 2-inch by 6-inch strips. Cut another piece that is 4-inches by 6-inches. Now make small cuts into each section.

Starting at the top of the paper towel tube, use tape to attach the larger strip, and then the smaller strips, wrapping each around the tube, with the cut segments facing all the same way.

You can color the "trunk" of the tree (the part with no paper attached) any way you like (with crayons and glitter), but keep in mind that the brown tube makes it look like bark.

Bad Words

Swearing is still bad, no matter which words you use.

Nor should there be obscenity.

~ Ephesians 5:4

Substitute Swear Words

"Why can't I say that?" asked Molly. "It's not a swear word." Molly had just said "crap." It wasn't exactly a bad word, but Molly said it in place of a word that she knew was bad to say.

"Even if it wasn't a swear word," answered Mommy, "you meant it to be one, so it was like swearing."

Molly thought about what Mommy said. It was true that she had used the word in place of a swear word so she wouldn't get into trouble. It felt good to do something bad without really being bad. Now she understood she shouldn't use bad words. She decided that she would try her best to never do so again, even if it was really hard sometimes not to.

Jesus doesn't want you to swear. He tells us in the Bible that we shouldn't ever use obscenities, which means bad words, or even have bad thoughts. Jesus wants you to be as good as you can be, and as much like Him as you can be.

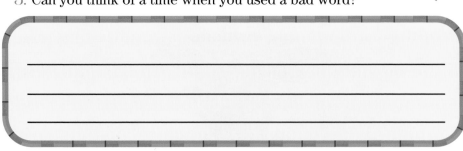

Your Turn

1. What did Molly say that was bad?
2. Why was the word she said bad, even if it wasn't a normal swear word?
3. Can you think of a time when you used a bad word?

Prayer

Jesus, please help me to never use bad words, or swear. Amen.

Missing Words

Jesus doesn't want you to use bad words, but He does want you to think about words and use them correctly.

Look at the picture of Molly—how do you think she is feeling?

What are some words you can when you are mad?

_____.

What are some things you could say instead of bad words?

_____.

Giving

Giving of what you have to help others is part of being a Christian.
Bring the best of the firstfruits of your soil to the house of the LORD.
~ Exodus 23:19

The Lost Dollar

Janelle watched the offering basket as it was passed person-to-person down the pews. This was one of her favorite parts of church. She always had her money out right away when the service started so that she would be ready when it was time for the offering. Now she could put her money in the basket, too! As the basket came her way, however, Janelle couldn't find her dollar. She must have lost it somewhere!

Janelle was starting to cry when Mommy leaned over and whispered, "It's OK. You can just give two dollars next Sunday." Janelle felt better then. She knew she could make it up next week.

I think Jesus would be happy with how Janelle felt. He wants you to be excited about giving. It's important that we give some of what we have to help those who are in need. Part of being a Christian is committing to help others.

Your Turn

1. Why was Janelle upset that she lost her dollar?
2. What's your favorite part of the church service?
3. Do you always give an offering in church?

Prayer

Jesus, I want to always give some of what I have to help others. Please help me remember how important that is. Amen.

Silly Signs

Jesus wants you to give some of what you have to help others. This activity is something you can share with your family and friends.

What you need:

1. Construction paper
2. Tape
3. Markers or crayons
4. Safety scissors (ask an adult for help)
5. Popsicle stick

What to do:

Cut a triangle out of cardboard. Decorate the triangle any way you like. Hold up the cardboard and tape a popsicle stick to it. Now, you have your own silly sign to share!

Reminders

Reminders of people can be both happy and sad.
Remember Jesus Christ.
~ 2 Timothy 2:8

Happy Reminders

"Why are you crying, Alexis?" asked Mrs. Curtis, Alexis' Sunday school teacher. Mrs. Curtis had seen Alexis run into the bathroom at church with tears in her eyes, and followed her to see what was wrong.

"My grandpa died in March," Alexis explained, "and this place reminds me of him. He had the same picture on the wall and the same name for his church. It makes me sad."

"But why does it make you sad?" asked Mrs. Curtis. "Doesn't it make you feel closer to him?"

Alexis thought about that. It was true. She was sad to have her grandpa gone, but it was kind of nice to be surrounded by things that reminded her of him.

When you think of how Jesus died on the cross, it can seem very sad too. But if we remember that Jesus died because He loves us, and that He was raised from the dead, then seeing the cross can be a happy thing as well. In the same way, having someone you love die can be very sad. However, when you see things that remind you of a loved one, why not be happy?

Your Turn

1. Why was Alexis crying?
2. What did Mrs. Curtis tell Alexis to make her feel better?
3. Can you think of something that reminds you of someone you love?

Prayer

Jesus, thank You for all the good reminders of people I love. Amen.

Rainbows

Jesus gives you many reminders of His love, like rainbows after a storm. I just love rainbows!

Color the rainbow below and remember God's great love for you!

Everyone is Different

Jesus is good for everyone, no matter who they are or what they like.

All the ways of the LORD are loving and faithful.
~ Psalm 25:10

The Missing Bird

"One of our birds is loose in the house," Mommy said when she picked Olivia up from daycare. "The first thing we have to do when we get home is find that bird."

Olivia could tell that Mommy was worried, but Olivia wasn't. All Olivia felt was happy and excited. It would be an adventure to catch a bird in the house!

When they got home, they began their search for the tiny bird. Olivia was laughing at first, but soon stopped when she saw how upset Mommy was. Mommy looked like she was either going to scream or cry if they didn't find the bird soon.

After several minutes of careful searching, Olivia was thrilled to see the bird sitting on one of the plants on the windowsill. Soon they had him back safely in his cage.

What is fun for one person is sometimes terrible for another. Olivia learned that while she thought having a bird loose in the house was wonderful, her Mommy didn't. You have to be careful when deciding what's good for someone, because everyone is different. The one thing that's good for everyone is Jesus!

Your Turn

1. What did Mommy tell Olivia when she picked her up from daycare?
2. Who was happy that the bird was loose? Who was not happy?
3. Can you think of something that is good for you, but not good for someone else?

Prayer

Jesus, thank You for being good for everyone. Amen.

Tissue Flowers

The joy of Jesus' love is the same for everyone. However, not everything is that way. What's fun for one person may not be fun for another.

Here's an activity that almost everyone will think is fun.

What you need:

1. Tissues
2. Twist ties or string

What to do:

Fold a tissue back and forth accordion style. Tie the tissue with string (or a twist tie) in the middle. Now, fold the two sides up together and fluff.

If you want a fuller, more fluffy "flower," use several tissues tied together so you have more layers to fluff in the final step.

Testing

Jesus' word is to be trusted, not tested.

Do not put the Lord your God to the test.

~ Matthew 4:7

Jesus Is the Answer

"How do we know that what the Bible says is true?" was just one of the many questions Miss Suzie heard the kids at Sunday School ask. She knew that the children all had questions, and she had a lot of the answers. But not all of them!

"You're going to learn a lot of the answers to your questions over the next few years as we study the Bible," Miss Suzie told the kids. "You need to pay attention when we read the Bible and keep asking questions so you'll understand who Jesus is and what it means to be a Christian."

"But why can't we get all of our questions answered right now?" asked one of the older children.

"Because a part of being a Christian is believing on faith," answered Miss Suzie. "You have to believe in Jesus enough to be willing to wait for the answers."

Part of being a Christian is trusting that Jesus is who the Bible says He is. It's good to ask questions and learn to understand Him the best that you can; just make sure you're trusting God, not testing Him.

Your Turn

1. What was Miss Suzie asked about?
2. How did Miss Suzie answer?
3. What questions do you have about God?

_____

_____

_____

_____

Prayer

Jesus, please help me to trust You as I ask questions and learn about my faith. Amen.

The Cross

It's OK to ask questions about Jesus. In fact, that's one of the best ways to learn about your faith.

Below is a picture of something that makes us think about our faith. Do you know what it is? You can connect the dots while you think about what the cross means to you!

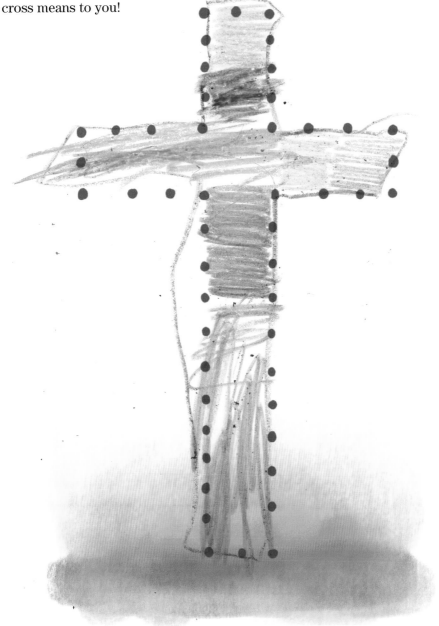

Being Sensitive

Be careful not to hurt other people, especially when they're sensitive.
A hot-tempered one commits many sins.
~ Proverbs 29:22

Hurt Feelings

"You wear training pants, so there!" Morgan yelled at her older sister Brooke. Morgan was mad because Brooke wouldn't play with her. Morgan wanted to hurt Brooke because Brooke wouldn't play with her, and so she said what she knew would upset her sister most. She teased Brooke about wearing training pants.

"Lots of older kids wear training pants," replied Brooke, with tears in her eyes. "It's a medical condition!" Brooke was already in school and still had accidents at night.

Brooke was sensitive about wearing training pants. That means it was something that made her extra sad to think about.

Jesus wants you to be especially careful when you know someone is sensitive about something. You should never use someone's sensitivity to make yourself feel better, like Morgan did.

Your Turn

1. What did Morgan say to Brooke?
2. Why did Morgan want to hurt Brooke?
3. Can you think of something that you're sensitive about?

Prayer

Jesus, please help me to be extra careful when I know someone is sensitive about something. Amen.

 Cardboard Flowers

Everyone is sensitive about something, so Jesus wants you to be careful not to hurt other people when they are already sad.

If you do ever hurt someone else, here's something you can make for them to help say you are sorry.

What you need:

1. Cardboard
2. Crayons
3. Glitter
4. Safety scissors

What to do:

Cut out two cardboard flowers as shown. Decorate the two flowers with your crayons and glitter. Place cut marks as indicated, and then slide one cardboard cut-out over the other. Now you have a pretty flower to give as a gift.

Humility

Jesus wants us all to be humble.

Whoever humbles himself...is the greatest in the kingdom of heaven.

~ Matthew 18:4

Mine's Better!

"Mine's better," said Elizabeth, as she showed Natalie her pink fuzzy scarf. Natalie had worn a red scarf just like it, but Elizabeth wanted to be sure everyone knew hers was better.

"No, mine's prettier," argued Natalie, as Elizabeth twirled around the room. "Mine's even hollow inside," shouted Natalie, "so I can put my hands inside it to keep them warm."

Suddenly, Kaylee ran up and said she had a fuzzy scarf that was even better than Natalie's or Elizabeth's. "Mine can be worn as a scarf or even a dress if I pull it over me."

It was never decided just who had the best scarf, but one thing was clear: all three girls had acted poorly. Each wanted to believe her scarf was the best, instead of being happy for the other girls. They were not being humble, but taking too much pride in their belongings.

Jesus wants you to be humble. Jesus loves you and thinks you're special, but He doesn't want you to act like you're better than other people. Jesus loves us all.

Your Turn

1. What were the three girls arguing about?
2. Who had the best scarf?
3. Are you always humble?

Prayer

Jesus, please help me to be humble and not put myself or my opinions ahead of others. Amen.

Which is Which?

Jesus doesn't want you to act like you're better than other people. In the activity below, Elizabeth and Natalie's fishing lines have gotten tangled. They're being humble—neither one is saying her fish is bigger or better—but they can't figure out whose fish is whose.

Can you follow the tangled lines to find which fish belongs to which girl?

Doing Right

Doing right brings God joy.

If you love me, you will obey what I command.
~ John 14:15

Giving Away Puppies

Jasmine was sitting next to the crate that had eight little white puppies in it. They were so cute. She wanted to keep them all, but Mommy was making her give them away to other people.

"They're going to get good homes," said Mommy. "And these little puppies will grow into big dogs like their mother." Mommy explained to Jasmine that it wouldn't be right to keep so many puppies since she couldn't take care of them.

Jasmine knew that they already had two dogs and that was enough, but it was hard to give the puppies away. As she held the tiny white puppies, Jasmine almost cried at the thought of watching someone else take them away.

Sometimes doing the right thing can be hard. It would have been more fun to see the puppies grow, but having more dogs when there wasn't room for them would be wrong. Jesus wants you to always do the right thing, even when it's tough.

Your Turn

1. What did Jasmine need to give away?
2. Why did the puppies need to be given away?
3. Can you remember a time when you had to do something difficult that you knew was right?

_____

_____

_____

_____

Prayer

Jesus, please help me to do what is right, especially when it's difficult. Amen.

Choose the Words

Jesus always wants you to do the right thing, but knowing what is right can sometimes be hard. When you need His help, you can always pray to Him, and He will make you strong.

The pictures below are symbols for words that will help you understand one of Jesus' promises. Can you and your mommy or daddy figure out the missing words and complete the special message?

Jesus _____ me.

He will always take care of _____.

I can _____ to Him and

He will always _____me.

Just the Way You Are

Jesus made us all beautiful.

Man looks at the outward appearance, but the LORD looks at the heart.

~ 1 Samuel 16:7

Jesus Makeup

"I wanted to be pretty," said Rebecca as tears streamed down her face. She had brought her makeup kit along with her in the car. Grandma had given it to her, and it had every type of makeup she could imagine. Rebecca had planned to put on makeup before she went into church, but when she opened the case, the lipstick she wanted was gone. "Now I won't be pretty!" she cried.

Mommy wiped Rebecca's face and hugged her tight. "You don't need makeup to be pretty," Mommy said.

"But I don't even have my red lipstick," sniffled Rebecca. She especially loved the bright red lipstick that was usually in the case.

"Can't you see that God made your lips a pretty red already?" answered Mommy. "He already made you beautiful in every way. You don't need anything else to make you beautiful."

Rebecca thought she needed makeup to look pretty, but she was wrong. Jesus made us all beautiful in our own special ways. You don't need anything else to be pretty. Jesus' love is already the best makeup that there is.

Your Turn

1. What did Rebecca bring with her in the car?
2. What was missing from the makeup kit?
3. What is one of the ways that Jesus made you special?

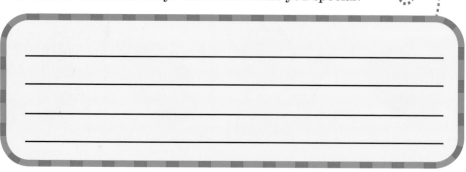

Prayer

Jesus, thank You for making me so beautiful and special. Amen.

Finger Flour

Jesus sees the real beauty inside each of us, and we are all beautiful in our own special ways. Here's something that's pretty and fun, but it really shows its beauty when you play with it.

What you need:

1. A clean tabletop or large cutting board
2. Flour

What to do:

This is a simple activity that taps into your creativity. Simply place a small amount of flour on the clean work surface (about one cup is all you need) and then use your fingers to make designs in it. If you have several types of flour with various colors and textures, that's even better.

Old Age

Old age is just another part of life.

Wisdom is with the aged, and understanding in length of days.

~ Job 12:12

Clarence the Gerbil

"Clarence is a really old gerbil, isn't he?" asked Abby one day.

"Yes, he is," answered Mommy. "He's the oldest gerbil I've ever had for a pet."

Clarence was a pretty golden-brown color, cute and fuzzy, but also old and chubby. He loved to chew up empty paper towel tubes, and ate sunflower seeds and popcorn every night. As he had grown old, Clarence slept most of the day, and sometimes walked quite slowly. Still, he seemed happy and content.

"He's old and can't do much anymore," said Abby. "He doesn't even want to run in the wheel or play with balls like he used to. Do you think he's happy?"

"Everyone gets old," said Mommy. "Someday I'll have to walk slow too and won't be able to do the things I do now, but that doesn't mean I won't be happy anymore. So, yes," added Mommy, "I think Clarence is very happy."

Even you will grow old someday, but that doesn't mean that you won't be happy anymore. Even when you can't do the same things you like to do now, you can still be happy. Growing old is just another part of God's plan for you.

Your Turn

1. Why was Abby worried about Clarence?

2. What was Clarence too old to do?

3. Are there some things you used to be able to do, but can't now that you're older/bigger?

Prayer

Jesus, thank You for letting me grow older so I can learn and do lots of different things. Amen.

Paper Snowflakes

Jesus designed you to grow old. It's a part of His plan for you to be able to do different things at different ages.

Here's something fun that you can enjoy making at any age, but it's best to do this with a grown-up: paper snowflakes! Grab a piece of white paper and a pair of scissors. To begin making your snowflake, fold your piece of paper in half and cut it into a semi-circle. Once it is cut, fold the paper in half again (it should look kind of like a slice of pizza). Now take your scissors and cut tiny sections out of the paper. You can make cuts and designs on all sides. When you are finished, unfold the paper and see your beautiful new snowflake!

* Note: There are many variations of these instructions. Experimenting is half the fun!

Importance

Don't waste time being upset over unimportant things.
Our days on earth are but a shadow.

~ Job 8:9

Will It Matter in Ten Years?

"Carly said my voice doesn't sound pretty," complained Jada. "She says my voice is too high." Jada was very proud of her singing voice and loved to sing whenever she could. It made her feel sad that her friend Carly didn't like her voice.

The next day, Jada and Carly were good friends once again, and played happily together. Carly even told Jada that she liked her voice after all. However, two days later Jada was still upset about Carly's comments. Jada just couldn't forget that Carly had said her voice was too high.

"Whenever something is bothering me," said Mommy, "I ask myself if it will matter 10 years from now. If it won't, then it's probably not worth being so upset about." Mommy looked into Jada's eyes and asked, "Do you think it will matter 10 years from now that Carly said she didn't like your voice?"

Jada thought about it and decided that Carly's one little comment really wasn't that important after all.

Why waste time being upset over things that aren't all that important? Carly was a good friend to Jada, so being upset over one little thing was foolish. Jesus wants you to enjoy your life and not waste time being upset over unimportant things.

Your Turn

1. What did Carly say to upset Jada?
2. Why was Jada upset by what Carly had said?
3. What was Mommy's advice for Jada?

Prayer

Jesus, please help me to not waste time being upset about things that are unimportant. Amen.

What's Important?

What seems important now may not be important later. Jesus wants you to keep in mind what's really important.

   Below are some pictures of things that are very important and some that are not. Circle the ones that are important and place an "X" through the ones that are less important.

Learning
God's Way

Bad Influences

We shouldn't be around people who are doing bad things.
What fellowship can light have with darkness?
~ 2 Corinthians 6:14

"It Wasn't Me!"

"But it wasn't me!" cried Ashley. "I wasn't saying bad words. It was the other girls who were." Ashley had been playing with two other girls who thought it was fun to say bad words over and over again. When they got in trouble, she did too.

"If you play with people who are doing bad things," explained Mommy, "then you will probably be blamed too."

"But that's not fair!" hollered Ashley.

Mommy gave Ashley a hug and said, "I know that you would never say bad words. But if you're with girls who do, people who don't know you like I do will think you're just the same as they are."

Jesus wants you to have fun playing with other children, but you need to remember that being with people who are doing bad things isn't a good idea.

Your Turn

1. What did Ashley get in trouble for?
2. Why did Ashley get in trouble even though she wasn't saying bad words?
3. Have you ever gotten in trouble for something that you didn't do just because someone you were with did a bad thing?

Prayer

Jesus, please help me to be smart about the friendship choices I make. Amen.

Good or Bad?

Jesus wants you to stay away from people who are doing bad things.

Below is a picture of two groups of kids. One group is doing something good and the other is doing something bad. Draw yourself in with the group playing well together.

Comfort

Jesus is always there to make you feel better.

I...am he who comforts you.

~ Isaiah 51:12

Scary Hospital

Sarah wasn't sure where she was. When she opened her eyes, she was in a room with a lot of doctors and nurses rushing around her. It looked like a hospital, and she was scared. The last thing she could remember was falling down and telling Mommy that her head hurt. What had happened?

Mommy was scared too. Sarah had fallen so hard that Mommy was afraid she might have hurt her brain.

While they waited for the test results to tell them if Sarah would be OK, Mommy decided to talk to Jesus. She prayed that Sarah would be well, and that God would give them all the strength and guidance they needed to get through this difficult situation. Sarah and Mommy felt better just knowing that Jesus was there with them, and that He was watching over what was happening. It brought a lot of comfort to them both.

Just like Sarah and her mommy, if you ever need comfort, you can always pray to Jesus. He will be by your side and can always make you feel better.

Your Turn

1. Why was Sarah in the hospital?
2. What did Mommy do to make them both feel better?
3. Do you ever pray to Jesus when you need comfort?

_____

_____

_____

_____

Prayer

Jesus, please help me to remember that You are always there to comfort me when I need You. Amen.

What Comes Next?

Jesus wants you to know that He is always there for you, no matter where you are or what happens. You can always feel better if you remember He is right by your side.

Here is a picture of Sarah in the hospital. Someone else is with her. Connect the dots to see who it is.

God's Name

Only use God's name when you're talking to, or about, Him.

You shall not misuse the name of the LORD.

~ Exodus 20:7

Oh My God!

Madison was confused. Mommy had told her that it was bad to say "Oh my God," but she had been hearing lots of people say it, and they didn't seem like bad people.

"Why do some people say that?" Madison asked Mommy one day.

"People say that for many reasons," Mommy explained. "Sometimes they say it because they don't know that it's a bad thing to say. Others may say it by accident, and some people just don't care that it's bad, or don't believe that it is."

"Is it ever OK to say it?" asked Madison.

"It's only OK to use God's name if you're speaking about Him or to Him," explained Mommy. "God's name shouldn't be used without thinking—He's too important for that."

Jesus wants you to use His name when you're talking about Him, or praying to Him. We should always think about what we say before we say it. It's important.

Your Turn

1. What saying was Madison confused about?
2. When is it OK to use God's name?
3. Do you ever use God's name in the wrong way?

Prayer

Jesus, please help me to never use Your name in the wrong way. Amen.

10 Commandments

One of Jesus' rules for your life is to never swear, or misuse His name. In fact, it's one of the Ten Commandments.

Below is a list of all of the Ten Commandments, plus two more that don't belong. Can you find the two that are made up?

You shall....

* ✳ have no other gods
* ✳ not swear
* ✳ eat cookies every day
* ✳ obey your Mommy and Daddy
* ✳ worship God
* ✳ not kill
* ✳ not commit adultery
* ✳ not be happy in church
* ✳ not steal
* ✳ not lie
* ✳ not want what others have

Belief

Belief in Jesus is the only way to be truly washed clean of your sins.

Whoever hears my word and believes…has eternal life.

~ John 5:24

Oily Hair

"I don't want my hair washed!" yelled Jocelyn. Mommy said that Jocelyn had oily hair and needed to clean it every day, but Jocelyn didn't like the feeling of having it washed. "You and Daddy rub too hard," she explained.

"Well, Jocelyn," Mommy answered, "if we don't rub the soap in well, it won't wash the oils out." Mommy then took her into the kitchen and had Jocelyn dip her finger into cooking oil and hold it under running water. "You see?" Mommy said. "The water alone won't take the oil away. You have to use the soap and rub it in well if you want the oil to come off."

Just like water alone wouldn't wash away the oil in Jocelyn's hair, the Bible tells you that no matter how many good things you do, you must believe in God. Belief is the only thing that will truly wash you clean of your sins.

Your Turn

1. Why did Jocelyn dislike having her hair washed?
2. How can your sins be washed away?
3. Do you believe in God?

Prayer

Jesus, please help me to remember that believing in You is the most important thing. Amen.

Confetti Bag

Belief in Jesus is the only thing that will truly wash you clean of your sins. This activity won't wash away your sins, but it is a lot of fun! Make sure you ask your parents where the best place to do this would be.

What you need:

1. Paper bag (lunch bag or small grocery-size bag)
2. Crayons
3. Confetti (you can buy some or just cut up your own)

What to do:

Decorate the bag any way you like with crayons. Fill it with confetti and secure with tape.

If using a large bag, hang it up and hit it with your fists until it breaks. If using a small bag, you can blow air into it before closing and then burst it between your hands. When the bag bursts, you'll be showered with fun!

Name Calling

It's wrong to call people bad names.
Nor should there be obscenity, foolish talk, or coarse joking.
~ Ephesians 5:4

Big, Fat, Meanie-Heads

"Sophie, you big, fat, meanie-head!" It was a terrible thing to hear yelled in the house, but it was a phrase that was being heard often in Taylor's home. Her little sister Isabel would yell it at her older sister Sophie whenever they got mad at each other.

One day Taylor decided that she had had enough. "Mommy," Taylor said, "I think it's really wrong of Isabel to call Sophie such a bad name." Taylor knew that Mommy had always scolded Isabel for saying such naughty things, but scolding hadn't made her stop. "You need to do something."

Mommy thought about what Taylor said and realized that she should have done something about the name-calling sooner. Even though Mommy scolded Isabel, that wasn't enough. From then on, Isabel had to do extra chores whenever she called people names.

Even mommies and daddies can make mistakes sometimes, so Taylor was right to point out the problem to her mommy. Name calling can be very hurtful to people, and it's not a nice thing to do. Jesus wants you to do your best to stop name calling whenever you can, just like Taylor did.

Your Turn

1. What did Isabel yell at her sister Sophie?
2. Why is it wrong to call people names?
3. Do you ever call people names?

Prayer

Jesus, please help me to never call people bad names. Amen.

Cornmeal Chips

Jesus doesn't want you to call people mean names. Proverbs 16:24 says, "Pleasant words are a honeycomb, sweet to the soul and healing to the bones." Here's a tasty recipe you can prepare with friends for a yummy treat.

What you need:

1. 1 cup cornmeal
2. 1 tbsp vegetable oil
3. ¾ tsp salt
4. ¾ cup boiling water
5. ⅛ cup of granulated sugar
6. 3-4 tbsp of ground cinnamon sugar
7. mixing bowl and spoon
8. baking sheet

What to do:

Mix the first five ingredients. It will require a lot of stirring until everything is well mixed. After it's all mixed, let the mixture just sit for a while (about 5 minutes). Spread (very thin) on greased baking sheet. We spread it in one, big even piece (and then break it apart after it cools), but you can do little sections or shapes if you like. Sprinkle with cinnamon sugar to taste.

With an adult's help, bake fifteen to twenty minutes at 400° Farenheit until the edges are brown.

*Note: you can experiment with different flavorings if you like. For instance, we sometimes use garlic powder or cayenne pepper, but you can try what works for you.

Obedience to Parents

Your parents know what's best.

Children, obey your parents in the Lord.

~ Ephesians 6:1

Bedtime Battles

"I don't want to go to bed!" cried Ava. She had just started to play with her favorite toy pony. Why did Mommy and Daddy always want her to go to bed so early? She wasn't tired at all!

Ava decided that she would just ignore her mom. Instead of going to bed, she would keep playing.

"Ava, why haven't you gone to bed yet?" Mommy asked. "You know it's bedtime."

Ava just kept playing.

Mommy picked up the pony and placed it on top of the refrigerator where Ava couldn't reach it. Her punishment for disobeying Mommy was to have her pony taken away for a whole day.

Jesus doesn't want you to act like Ava did. He gave you parents to take care of you, so you should obey them. Ava's mommy knew how much sleep Ava's body needed. Ava should have gone to bed because it was what was best for her.

Your Turn

1. What was Ava supposed to do?
2. What did Ava do that was wrong?
3. Can you remember a time when you disobeyed your parents?

_____

_____

_____

_____

Prayer

Jesus, thank You for giving me my parents. Please help me to always obey them. Amen.

Love and Obey

Everyone needs to learn obedience—even your mommy and daddy had to learn how to obey. Jesus wants you to obey your parents because He gave them the big job of taking care of you and helping you as you grow up.

Ava didn't want to go to bed. She was disobeying her parents. The Bible tells us that we show our love for God—and mommies and daddies—by obeying. Below are the words "LOVE" and "OBEY." See how they are connected? Think about it as you finish coloring the letters.

Unbelievers

Not everyone knows about Jesus yet.

See to it...that none of you has a sinful, unbelieving heart.

~ Hebrews 3:12

Finding Jesus

"Why doesn't Amy believe in God?" asked Chloe. "She never goes to church." Amy was a little girl at Chloe's preschool with whom she liked to play.

"I think her family just hasn't found Jesus yet," Mommy answered.

Chloe looked confused and asked, "Do you mean Jesus got lost?"

"No, honey," Mommy chuckled. "Sometimes people get lost. Not everyone knows Jesus from when they're little like you. Sometimes it takes a while for them to learn about Jesus and understand Him."

"Does that mean Amy is bad?" asked Chloe.

"No, it doesn't mean she's bad," said Mommy.

"Do you think Amy will find Jesus soon?" Chloe asked.

"I don't know," Mommy frowned. "But if you tell Amy about Jesus it might help."

Not everyone knows about Jesus. Sometimes it takes many years before a person comes to believe in Jesus like you do. People who don't believe aren't bad—they just still need to meet Jesus and discover His amazing love for them. You can help with that by telling people what you know about Him.

Your Turn

1. Did Chloe's friend believe in Jesus?
2. Why didn't Chloe's friend believe in Jesus?
3. Can you think of some ways that Chloe could help her friend to know Jesus?

Prayer

Jesus, help me to remember that people who don't believe in You aren't bad. Please show me how to help others learn about You. Amen.

Bible Bookmarks

Not everyone knows about Jesus, so Jesus wants you to tell people about Him. One way to do that is with this activity. You can make these Bible bookmarks and give them to friends and to people who may not know about Jesus.

What you need:

1. Stiff paper or thin cardboard
2. Crayons
3. Safety scissors

What to do:

Lay out your piece of paper or cardboard, and outline the shape of your bookmarks (you can make more than one out of a single sheet). Decorate the bookmarks any way you like, but be sure to include a religious symbol or a Bible verse on each of them. When you're done, have a grown-up cut out the bookmarks for you.

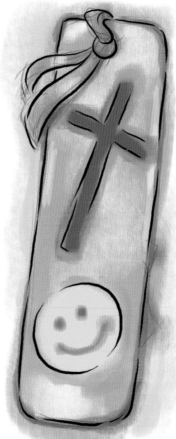

Christmas

Remember that Christmas is about Jesus.

She will give birth to a son, and you are to give him the name Jesus,
because he will save his people from their sins.

~ Matthew 1:21

What Christmas is About

"I just want to get past Christmas," said Mommy with a sigh. It had taken a lot of time to get ready for the holiday. Sydney had helped wrap presents, bake cookies and hand out treats, and it seemed like lots of fun to her.

"Why do you want Christmas to be over?" asked Sydney.

"Because it's a lot of work," answered Mommy.

Sydney didn't understand why Mommy wouldn't like it. "Christmas is wonderful. It's when Jesus was born. You should want it to be Christmas all the time!" she said.

Sometimes people can forget what's important about Christmas. They get so caught up in all the things people do for the holidays that it can seem like extra work instead of a joy.

Jesus wants you to have fun at Christmas time. Presents, Christmas cookies, caroling, and all those other fun things are great, but the most important part of Christmas is Jesus' birth.

Your Turn

1. Why did Sydney's mommy want Christmas to be over?
2. What is the most important thing about Christmas?
3. What's your favorite thing to do at Christmastime?

Prayer

Jesus, please help me to always remember that Christmas isn't about presents and cookies, but about celebrating You. Amen.

Window Hangings

Jesus wants you to have fun at Christmas—it's when we celebrate His birthday! Jesus helps us to see God's love all around us. You can make these window hangings to put up at home as a reminder of Jesus' gift to us.

What you need:

1. Coffee filter
2. Markers
3. Water
4. Parchment paper
5. Safety scissors
6. Glue

What to do:

Cut the parchment paper into whatever shape you want your window hanging to be. Then, color the coffee filter with the markers. If you just hold the tip of the markers to the filter, the color will leak out. Experiment and you will find fun ways to do it. Next, wet the filter with water. Press the filter to the parchment paper, and secure it with a thin layer of glue. Lay your hanging on a flat surface, place a heavy book on top, and let it dry.

When it's ready, place your lovely creation in the window and enjoy all the beautiful colors!

The Bible

Try to learn about the Bible whenever you can.
Hold on to instruction, do not let it go.

~ Proverbs 4:13

Learning God's Word

"I want to go again," said Skylar with excitement. "I loved it!" Skylar had just come from a special Bible class that a friend's church was holding for children.

"I don't know," said Mommy. "We already do a whole lot." Mommy didn't like the idea of adding another activity to the family schedule. They were already so busy.

"But I learned so much," said Skylar. "Listen to what I learned." As Mommy listened, Skylar said a Bible verse that she had memorized all by herself. When Mommy heard that, she made up her mind to let Skylar go again.

Skylar's mommy didn't want to be busier than she already was, but hearing the Bible verse reminded her of how important it is to learn God's word.

Jesus wants you to always learn more of the words He gave you in the Bible. It's one of the most important things you can do—far more important than the other activities that may keep you busy. Jesus would have been proud of Skylar and her desire to learn more of His word. He would have been proud of Skylar's mommy, too, for realizing that having her daughter learn about the Bible was worth setting aside some extra time.

Your Turn

1. What did Skylar want to do?
2. Why was Mommy unsure if Skylar should go to the Bible class?
3. Do you have a time set aside for learning about the Bible?

Prayer

Jesus, help me to remember how important it is to learn about the Bible. Amen.

Pick A Stick

Jesus wants you to learn about the Bible. In fact, He wants you to learn as much as you can. Here's an activity where you can learn something new about the Bible.

What you need:

1. Craft sticks
2. Paper
3. Tape
4. Crayons
5. Cup

What to do:

Cut the paper into five 2"x 2" pieces. On each of the squares, draw a picture: a snake, an apple, a cross, a fish, and a light.

Tape each paper square to the end of a craft stick and place them, picture first, into the cup.

Take turns with your mommy or daddy drawing a stick from the cup. When you "pick a stick," you must explain why the picture has something to do with the Bible. You can make more stick pictures if you'd like to play with more people.

Politeness

You should always be polite.

*By this all men will know that you are
my disciples, if you love one another.*

~ John 13:35

The Bible Tells What God Is Like

The party was such fun! Amanda loved seeing her relatives, playing with her cousins and singing "Happy Birthday" to Uncle Harold.

Amanda tried to guess Uncle Harold's age. She couldn't believe it when she heard that he was eighty years old! He was ancient! Amanda didn't even know someone could be that old.

Amanda walked up to Aunt Selma (Uncle Harold's wife) and asked, "Aunt Selma, how come you're married to such an old man?" For some reason, Aunt Selma thought that was a very funny question, and she laughed and laughed as she told other people what Amanda had said.

Even though there was nothing wrong with Amanda's question, it was not a polite one. It's not polite to call someone an "old man." In Amanda's case, however, the people who heard it thought it was cute and funny, because she had said it. Jesus wants you to pay close attention to what is and isn't polite, so that you never hurt the feelings of other people.

Your Turn

1. What did Amanda ask Aunt Selma?
2. Why is it not a good idea to call someone an "old man"?
3. Do you ever say things that aren't polite?

_____

_____

_____

_____

Prayer

Jesus, help me to learn about being polite. Amen.

Bible Scrolls

Jesus wants you to learn lots of things, including how to be polite. You'll certainly learn something new with this activity!

What you need:
1. Two 12-inch rulers (or sticks)
2. Paper towels or long paper
3. Tape
4. Crayons or markers

What to do:
Unroll a length of paper towels; make it as long you'd like your "scroll" to be. I usually use about four feet.

Wrap each end of the paper towels around a ruler and tape them securely. Then, carefully roll each ruler toward the center, so that they meet in the middle.

You can use a pen to carefully draw some pictures on the scroll. Spend a few minutes discussing how scrolls were like books in the days of the Bible. Exodus 17:13-15 describes how God told Moses to write on a scroll. You can use this story in your discussion if you like.

Value

Value can't always be measured in dollars and cents.

*I consider everything a loss compared
to the surpassing greatness of knowing Christ Jesus.*

~ Philippians 3:8

The Old Ring

Trinity loved to look at Mommy's wedding ring. Mommy never took it off unless Trinity begged her to, so it was a special moment when she was able to hold it in her hands. She loved to run her finger across the smooth surface of the shiny, gold band, and try to fit it on her fingers.

One night, just before bed, Mommy let Trinity try her wedding band on again. But this time, when Trinity ran her finger across the surface, she noticed something that she hadn't seen before. There were lots of tiny scratches and grooves all over it.

"Your ring isn't as shiny any more, Mommy. Maybe you should get a new one."

But Mommy liked all the scratches and wear on her ring because it reminded her of how much life she had lived with Daddy, and how much they loved each other.

Some things are worth more to a person when they're old and used. Some of the best things in life, like parents, friends, and Jesus' love, are priceless, too.

Your Turn

1. What did Trinity like to look at?
2. Why did Trinity think Mommy needed a new ring?
3. Can you think of some things that wouldn't be worth much to other people, but are worth a lot to you?

Prayer

Jesus, thank You for all the priceless gifts You give to me in my life. Amen.

Old Value

It isn't just brand new things that are worthwhile. Some things are just as valuable, or even more so, when they're old. Jesus gave us time, and ways to tell what time it is, but time doesn't tell us how much value something has.

Below are some things that are wonderful even when they're old. Color the pictures, and then tell someone why each is great whether it's old or new.

Living

God used His power to create animals.

Cry aloud for understanding.

~ Proverbs 2:3

Stuffed Animals Aren't Real

"I can't find Teddy," cried Rachel. "I can't go to bed without him."

"It's OK, Rachel," Mommy said. "He's probably just having a sleepover with his friends tonight. You'll find him tomorrow."

"Mommy, that's silly," said Rachel. "Teddy isn't real in that way. He can feel when I hug him, and he can make me feel better, but he's not real."

Rachel thought about it for a while. It was hard to accept that her Teddy bear wasn't alive because she loved him so much, but she knew it had to be true. Rachel knew that Teddy made her feel better, but he was still just a "thing."

Even though you may love your stuffed animals and toys, they aren't really alive. They may be soft and huggable, but they aren't alive like you or your friends. They are just things. Jesus wants you to be able to tell the difference between what's living and what isn't, because living things are much more important.

Your Turn

1. What was Rachel unable to find?
2. Was Teddy real? Is Teddy alive?
3. Do your toys sometimes seem like they're alive to you?

Prayer

Jesus, thank You for all my wonderful toys and stuffed animals. Help me to remember that they aren't alive like I am. Amen.

Leaf Rubbings

Jesus wants you to know what's living and what isn't.

This activity involves a little piece of nature. First, collect a few freshly picked leaves; try to get different kinds. Then, take the leaves inside and grab some white paper and a pencil or crayons. Before you begin this next part, ask yourself this question: are these leaves living, or not? Now, place a sheet of paper over one of the leaves. Press down securely, rub your pencil or crayon over the paper. Use the side of the crayon/pencil rather than the tip. You'll soon see the image of the leaf appear! Ask your parents for help.

Control

Trust Jesus to control everything around you.
Submit yourselves, then, to God.
~ James 4:7

Killing Time

Jennifer was bored. She didn't feel like playing with her toys or watching television. She didn't feel like playing with her brother or sisters. She didn't even want to play video games. Jennifer didn't feel like doing anything at all, so she simply sat on the front porch and watched the cars drive by.

"What are you doing?" asked her older brother Mark as he sat down beside her.

"Just killing time," Jennifer answered.

"You can't kill time," Mark said. "You can't control that."

"Oh yeah?" giggled Jennifer. "What if someone got rid of all the clocks?"

"Now you're just being silly," Mark said. "Even if you got rid of all the clocks, time still keeps moving."

Mark was right. Jennifer was being very silly. There are many things you can't control, and time is one of them. Only Jesus can control time—He controls everything. No matter what you do, or how hard you try, Jesus is still in control. He loves you, so you can trust Him to be in control.

Your Turn

1. What did Jennifer say she was doing?
2. Why can't Jennifer control time?
3. Are there some things you wish you could control?

Prayer

Jesus, I trust You to control the world and take care of me. Amen.

Bible Bread

Jesus is always in control, no matter what is happening in your life, or the world. Even if you're doing an everyday activity like baking bread, Jesus is there with you, keeping watch over you. Remember that as you have fun with this activity.

What you need:

1. 3 tbsp vegetable oil
2. 2 ¼ cups water
3. 1 tsp salt
4. 5 cups flour

What to do:

In a large bowl, mix the flour and salt. In a smaller bowl, combine the oil and water. Pour the liquid into the larger bowl of dry items and mix well. Let set for 30 minutes, then knead and roll the dough into small balls and flatten. We usually keep ours to about six inches in diameter and less than ¼ inch thick. Don't worry about over-kneading the dough—that's one of the most fun parts of the recipe!

Your mom or dad can fry the dough in a lightly oiled skillet until golden brown (about 6-8 minutes).

*Note: Parents, while you enjoy eating this treat you can discuss how unleavened bread played a role at the first Passover and in other Bible stories.

Sickness

Everyone gets sick sometimes.

Heal me, O LORD, and I will be healed.

~ Jeremiah 17:14

The Nose Cold

Kylie's teacher was laughing when she spoke to Mommy. "I don't remember what she called how she was feeling, but I'd never heard it before," the teacher said. Kylie had stayed home sick that day. Her nose was all red and she couldn't breathe through it because it was all stuffed up.

"Did she call it a nose cold?" Mommy asked.

"That's it!" said the teacher, laughing.

Mommy explained, "That's what Kylie calls it when she gets a cold, because it seems like she's only sick in that one area of her body."

Kylie had a cute name for when she had a cold. Even if you don't have a cute name for it, you'll get sick sometimes too. No matter how hard you try to avoid germs, or how careful you are to eat healthy foods and do healthy things, you will still get sick sometimes. It doesn't feel good, and it can be scary, but getting sick now and then is just a part of being alive, so it's OK. No matter how sick you get, you can trust Jesus to care for you. He loves you whether you're sick or well, and He is always watching over you.

Your Turn

1. Why did Kylie stay home from school?
2. What did Kylie call her illness?
3. Do you ever get sick?

_____

_____

_____

_____

Prayer

Jesus, thank You for watching over me always, even when I'm sick. Amen.

Feeling Better

Getting sick is just a part of being alive. It's not fun to be sick, but it can help to remember that Jesus will be with you no matter how you feel.

Below are some pictures of things that will help Kylie feel better when she's sick. Circle the ones that can make you feel better too. You can have more than one favorite!

Special Ways

Everyone is a little different, and that's OK.

We have different gifts, according to the grace given us.

~ Romans 12:6

God's Plans for My Life

"Is it good morning?" Makayla asked every day when she woke up. Even though most people just said "good morning," it was her special way of saying it.

"Don't you mean good morning?" Daddy asked.

"No, I mean it that way," answered Makayla.

A little later that afternoon, Daddy heard Makayla singing a song. He knew the tune, but the words were different from the ones he always sang.

The next day, Makayla saw Daddy put sugar on his toast. He always ate his toast that way and Mommy never did.

Everyone has their own ways of saying or doing certain things. Some ways are silly and some are special, but there's nothing wrong with doing things differently as long as you know the correct way, too. Jesus wants you to learn to do things the right way, but He doesn't mind if you're silly sometimes. Doing things differently from others is a part of what makes you like no one else. Jesus wants you to be your own special person.

Your Turn

1. How did Makayla greet people in the morning?
2. How did Makayla's daddy eat his toast?
3. What are some things that you do differently from everyone else?

Prayer

Jesus, thank You for making me my own special person, unlike anyone else. Amen.

Stepping Stones

Jesus wants you to be your own special person. As you grow, you will change. That's one of the reasons people take pictures of you—they want to remember what you looked like when you were little. This activity does the same thing, only in a different way. Moms and dads need to help with this project since it has special parts.

What you need:

1. Concrete mix (it comes in big bags, but is inexpensive)
2. Molds (old pie tins work great, but even shallow cardboard boxes will do)
3. Decorations (marbles, small stones, etc.)
4. Bucket
5. Shovel
6. Water

What to do:

This is so simple to do! Simply add the water to the concrete mix according to the instructions on the bag. Fill your mold with the wet cement, smoothing the top with your hands and shovel.

Now you're ready to decorate! Press small stones, charms, marbles, shells, and anything else you want into the concrete. You can even make a hand print, or use a stick to write your name.

Let your creation stand for 24 to 48 hours before taking it out of the mold. Now you have a unique stepping stone for your garden!

Tips for Moms and Dads:

* Cement has a drying effect on skin. Use gloves, or wash up immediately after.
* When you pour the concrete mix, it emits a fine dust. I just work outside, but you may want to wear a mask or stand back a bit for this part.
* It's best to have your mold be at least 3-4 inches in depth.
* Bring your stone inside for the winter.

Foolishness

We shouldn't do things that are foolish.
Make level paths for your feet.
~ Hebrews 12:13

Exploding Mess

Mommy wondered what the kids were doing. Every so often, she would see them run into the kitchen, grab something, then run off. They took spices, soda pop, ketchup, and lots of other things. As she watched more closely, Mommy noticed that they were taking the items outside.

"What are you doing?" Mommy finally asked when one of them came back in for another item.

"We're putting lots of stuff together into a bottle. We want to make it explode!"

As soon as Mommy heard that she went outside to see what they had made. There, outside on the lawn, was an ugly, smelly, yucky mixture of all kinds of things from the kitchen. It wasn't going to explode, but it was foolish of the kids to try to make something that could be dangerous.

Jesus wants you to have fun, but you shouldn't do things that are foolish. Doing things that are dangerous could hurt you and others, and that isn't good.

Your Turn

1. Why were the kids getting lots of things from the kitchen?
2. Was it good to try to make an explosion?
3. Can you think of something you once did that was foolish?

Prayer

Jesus, please help me to always make good choices so that I don't do anything that's foolish. Amen.

Rocket Canister

Jesus doesn't want you to do things that are foolish. Here's something you can do that is just exploding with fun! It may seem a little foolish, but I think you'll have a blast if you follow the instructions and only do it with an adult's help.

What you need:

1. Empty film canister (or other small, capped container)
2. Baking power (enough to fill your container half-way)
3. Vinegar (enough to fill the canister)

What to do:

Fill your canister a little less than half-full with baking powder. Add vinegar until container is about ¾ full. Depending upon the size of your container, the amounts of baking powder to vinegar are roughly 3 parts baking power to 1 part vinegar. Quickly cap the container, set the container on a flat surface, and step back. The contents will spray out, so keep back—you may even want to do this one outside.

If you place the container on the flat surface with the cap upward, you will be treated to a spray. If cap down, the entire container will fly into the air. A film canister really works well for this because it is small, light, and cylindrical. However, many containers will work, and experimenting is a lot of fun!

Chores

You should always do your share.
Whatever you do, work at it with all your heart.
~ Colossians 3:23

Little Bo Peep

"Look at me, look at me," called Hailey. She had tried on a costume and was dancing around the living room in the pretty white dress with ruffles and lace.

"Aren't you supposed to be doing your chores right now?" Mommy asked. It was Hailey's job to pick up her toys and dust off the furniture. Instead, she was playing.

"I can't work," answered Hailey. "I'm Little Bo Peep."

"Hailey," Mommy said in a stern voice, "do your chores now or you'll be in big trouble."

Stomping her foot, Hailey yelled, "I'm Little Bo Peep and I lost my sheep!"

Hailey continued to stomp around the living room, playing out her role of Little Bo Peep, happily avoiding what she was supposed to be doing in the house to help out, and she got in trouble for not obeying.

It's not OK to try to get out of doing your chores. Hailey thought she could use a silly excuse to avoid doing her share of the housework, but Jesus wouldn't want that. Jesus wants you to always do your share.

Your Turn

1. What did Hailey dress up as?
2. Why did Hailey think she shouldn't have to do her share of the chores?
3. What do you do at home to help out?

Prayer

Jesus, help me to always happily do my chores. Amen.

Oatmeal Feeder

Jesus wants you to do your chores. He wants you to do your share and be a helpful person. Hailey didn't want to do her chores because they weren't as fun as playing dress up, but not all chores are boring.

Here's a fun activity that's not a chore to do at all. It only takes a little work to make this bird feeder, and then you'll have hours of fun watching the birds come for a snack. You'll need your parent's help for this!

What you need:

1. Empty oatmeal container
2. Foil
3. Tape
4. String
5. Two plastic flying disks, five inches in diameter
6. Bird seed/oatmeal mixture
7. Drill
8. Caulk or glue

What to do:

Cut a small section (about 2x2 inches) from two opposite bottom sides of the oatmeal container (as shown in diagram 1). Wrap the outside of the container in foil and secure with tape. This will help protect the container from the elements as well as reflect the sun and fascinate the birds.

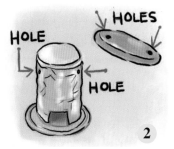

Apply glue or caulk (caulk works best) to the bottom end of the container and place it in the center of one of the flying disks (lip up). Let dry.

Drill holes on either side of the second flying disk and on the open end of the container (see diagram 2).

Cut a 20-inch length of string and thread it through the container and flying disk (as shown in diagram 3). The flying disk should be lip-down. Fill the container half-full with bird seed/oatmeal and slide the flying disk down to securely cover the opening.

Now you're ready to hang your feeder outside.

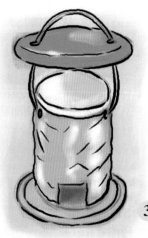

*Note: The diameter of a large oatmeal container is about five inches, and the flying disks we use are the five-inch type. If you can't find any disks that small, you can use a larger version.

Reasons

There can be more than one explanation for why things happen.

Counsel and sound judgement are mine.

~ Proverbs 8:14

The Sensitive Plant

Mommy had a brand new plant. She told the children that they would really like this one, so Mackenzie was the first to run up and see it. It was called a "Sensitive Plant."

"Why is it called a Sensitive Plant?" asked Mackenzie.

"Because when you touch its leaves, they curl up as if they don't like being touched," answered Mommy.

How exciting! Mackenzie couldn't wait to try it, and when she did, the leaves curled up just like Mommy said they would. "I know why it does that," said Mackenzie. "It's because of mosquitoes. It doesn't want to get bitten."

"That could be," said Mommy. "If it feels the mosquito land on it, it would want to curl up."

There are several possible reasons for why Mommy's new plant acts like it does, and Mackenzie's reason was a good guess. There can be more than one reason for why things happen, though. Jesus made a wonderful world for us to live in. It's not a simple world, but rather one that has many parts to it. Mackenzie knew that, and came up with a smart reason for the plant's behavior.

Your Turn

1. What was Mommy's new plant called?
2. Why did Mackenzie think it was called a Sensitive Plant?
3. Are you good at thinking up reasons for things?

_____

_____

_____

_____

Prayer

Jesus, thanks for making such a fun world for me to live in. Amen.

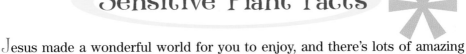

Sensitive Plant Facts

Jesus made a wonderful world for you to enjoy, and there's lots of amazing information out there to help you learn about it.

Below is a drawing of a Sensitive Plant. There are several explanations for why its leaves curl up. Circle the reasons you think are true and put an "X" over the ones you think aren't true.

Why do sensitive plants sometimes curl their leaves up?

* At night it curls up because there's no light.

* It's scared.

* It wants to surprise people.

* Because it gets cold sometimes.

* It thinks it's funny.

* To keep animals from eating it.

Hearing Bad Things

People who don't know Jesus sometimes say bad things about Him.

Men speak abusively against whatever they do not understand.

~ Jude 1:10

Lauren's Confusion

"Why does Lauren say church is stupid?" asked Sarah one night. "She said that her family doesn't go to church and that it's boring."

Mommy sat down beside Sarah and explained, "Maybe the reason Lauren thinks church is stupid is because she doesn't go."

"What do you mean?" asked Sarah.

"If she doesn't understand what church is all about, then that may be why she says bad things about it," said Mommy. "If Lauren understood who Jesus is, and how much He loves her, she might not say that church is stupid."

What Mommy said made sense to Sarah. She loved Jesus, so it was hard to hear bad things said about church. Lauren must just be confused about who Jesus is and what church means.

It can be hard to hear those bad things, but just remember that you know the truth. It can take a while for people who don't know about Jesus to really understand Him and what church is all about. You can help by telling others why you love Jesus and showing them how great it is to know Him.

Your Turn

1. What did Lauren say about church?
2. Why do you think Lauren said those things?
3. Have you ever heard someone say something bad about church?

Prayer

Jesus, please help me to remember that people who say bad things about You simply may not know You yet. Amen.

Maze

Some people don't know Jesus yet, or they don't understand Him. That's why you need to help those people learn about Jesus.

Sarah needs to help Lauren find Jesus. They're going to enter the maze together and walk by some things that can help Lauren find Him. Maybe you can help them too?

Idols

We should never bow to false gods, even if just in play.

Do not make idols.

~ Leviticus 26:1

False Gods

Victoria and her sisters were playing in the basement. They were pretending to be ancient people from long, long ago. They pretended to make a place to sleep out of sticks and blankets. They made imaginary soup in a big pot. Then they decided to pretend that they were worshiping an ancient god. They bowed and sang songs, just like they imagined people long ago might have.

When Mommy saw what the children were doing, she didn't like it. She explained that worshiping any god other than Jesus was very wrong. "But we're only pretending," said Victoria. "We don't mean it."

"As Christians," Mommy said, "we really shouldn't even pretend to do such things, because it is very serious."

The very first Commandment is that we should not have any gods other than Jesus, so it must be very important.

Your Turn

1. What was Victoria playing in the basement?
2. Why was pretending to bow to a false god a bad thing to do?
3. What do you think about what Victoria and her sisters did?.

Prayer

Jesus, please help me to remember that I should never bow to false gods of any kind. Amen.

Ice Cream Bag

You should only worship Jesus, no matter how wonderful something else might seem.

Here's a fun activity you can do with your parents that would have been much nicer for Victoria and her sisters to play with. It's so delicious, you won't even need to pretend you like it!

What you need:

1. Two large, sealable plastic bags
2. Two small, sealable plastic bags
3. ½ cup milk (we use skim milk)
4. 1 ¾ tbsp sugar
5. 2 cups of ice
6. ¼ tsp vanilla
7. 7 tbsp salt
8. Gloves (or oven mitts)

What to do:

* Double bag your large bags (to prevent leaks). Place ice and salt in large bag.
* Double bag your small bags. Place milk, sugar and vanilla in small bag.

* Seal the small bags and put them inside the large bags. Seal the large bags.

* Shake for approximately 10-12 minutes. Be sure to wear your gloves so your hands won't get too cold.

* Open the bag and enjoy. Yum, yum!

Your Body Grows

Everyone's body grows at a different speed.
The LORD will fulfill His purpose for me.

~ Psalm 138:8

The Late Nines

Jenna's teeth hurt. They had started to hurt way in the back of her mouth just a couple days before. Jenna tried to avoid chewing with those teeth. She even tried to hold her mouth still. No matter what she did, they still hurt.

Jenna asked Mommy about her teeth, but Mommy just said it was normal for new teeth to hurt a little sometimes as they came all the way out to where they needed to be.

"It's OK," said Mommy. "That's just your back teeth. Daddy said he got his in his late twenties, so you're just early. They're supposed to hurt, so you don't need to worry about it."

"Did you get your back teeth early?" asked Jenna.

"I got mine in my late nines," answered Mommy.

Everyone's body grows at a little different speed. Jenna's daddy got his back teeth at a different time than she did, and that's OK. Jesus has a plan for you and your body, and He will decide how quickly—or slowly—you should grow.

Your Turn

1. What was bothering Jenna?
2. What did Jenna's mother tell her?
3. Is there something about you that has grown faster or slower than your friends?

Prayer

Jesus, thank You for giving me a body that grows and changes. Amen.

Fruits and Vegetables

Jesus made our bodies so that they each grow at their own rate. Jesus wants you to take good care of the body He has given you, and one way to do that is by eating right.

Fruits and vegetables are good for your body, but sometimes it's hard to tell the difference between them. For example, lots of people think that a tomato is a vegetable, but it's really a fruit.

Can you tell what the rest of the fruits and vegetables are below? Draw a circle around the fruits and a square around the vegetables.

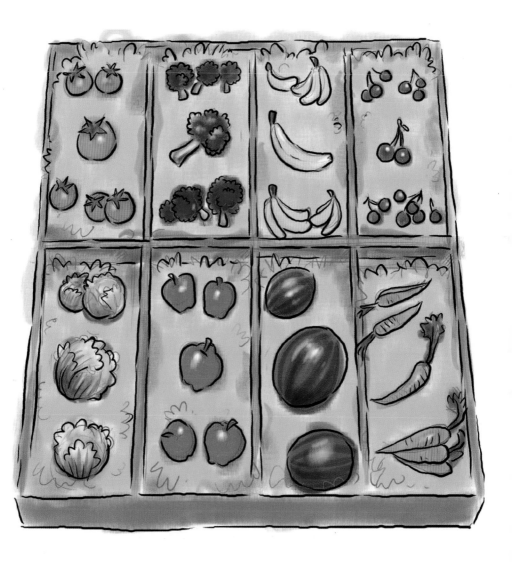

Wants

What we want isn't what we need.

Set your minds on things above.

~ Colossians 3:2

Pretty Kitty

Rochelle really wanted the pretend kitty at the store. It was the size of a real cat, all white and fluffy. The kitty was soft and cuddly, but the best thing about it was that it purred and meowed.

When Rochelle finally got her chance to go to the store, she was worried. What if someone else got to the kitty before she did? What if someone else had bought it already?

"You know, even if you don't get the kitty it's OK," Mommy told her.

"Why is that?" asked Rochelle.

"Because you already have a lot of stuffed animals. You don't really need another one, and some other little girl might need that kitty more," explained Mommy. "So if the kitty is already gone, you really don't need to be sad."

Rochelle thought about it and decided that if she couldn't get the kitty, she wouldn't be too upset. Maybe Mommy was right and some other little girl needed the kitty to cuddle more than she did.

Rochelle did get the kitty, and was thrilled to take it home with her. Jesus wants you to be happy and have nice things, but He also wants you to know the difference between what you need and what you simply want.

Your Turn

1. What did Rochelle want to buy?
2. Why would it be OK if Rochelle didn't get the kitty?
3. Can you give an example of something that you need, and something that you want?

_____

_____

_____

Prayer

Jesus, help me to remember that there's a difference between what I want and what I need. Amen.

Wants vs. Needs

Jesus wants you to know the difference between what you want and what you need. They can be very different things.

Below is a picture of a house filled with many things. Some are things you need and others are things you just want. Can you tell the difference? Color in the items you need.

Support

Jesus is there for us in times of trouble.
The Spirit helps us in our weakness.
~ Romans 8:26

Maria Helps

The room was dark where the little girl lay in the hospital bed. Maria was in the next bed. Maria had just had her appendix out and her tummy hurt. She heard the nurse say that the other little girl had also had her appendix out.

As Maria lay on her bed thinking about how bad her tummy hurt, she noticed the little girl next to her trying to reach for the cup of water on the bedside table. The little girl couldn't reach it, so Maria started to slowly ease her way down to the end of the bed. Maria didn't want to lie there without helping the other little girl.

Maria waited until she was sure there was no one coming down the hall. Then she eased off the end of the bed and hobbled over to the other girl's cup. Maria's tummy hurt a lot, but she felt so good inside when she was able to finally give the little girl a drink of water.

Even though it was hard for Maria, she still helped the other girl. Jesus wants us to help each other whenever we can.

Your Turn

1. Why was Maria in the hospital?
2. Why did Maria leave her bed?
3. Can you remember a time when you helped?

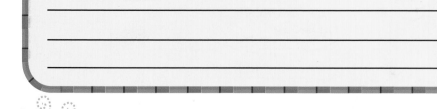

Prayer

Jesus, please help me to help others. Amen.

Berry Butter

Jesus wants you to help others whenever you can.

Here's something you can make to help your parents prepare supper. It can be a special treat for your family.

What you need:

1. ½ stick of butter, softened
2. Small squirt of lime juice
3. 1 tsp brown sugar
4. Mashed berries (we like strawberries or raspberries)

What to do:

Mix all of the ingredients together until smooth. The butter is even better if beaten for two to three minutes with a mixer!

Refrigerate so the butter can harden again, then enjoy!

Dealing with Pain

Jesus gives each of us a different ability to deal with pain.
He gives strength to the weary.
~ Isaiah 40:29

It Hurt For Me!

Lily had to get her stitches out, and she was scared. Everyone said that getting the stitches out would be a lot easier than having them put in, but Lily wasn't so sure.

A couple weeks before, Lily had fallen and cut her knee. She had gone to the hospital and got seven stitches to close the cut back up! Now the cut had healed and it was time to take the stitches out.

Daddy told Lily that he had stitches out once and it didn't hurt at all. He said it would be fine. However, when the doctor pulled the first stitch out, Lily didn't like how it felt.

When it was over, Lily's daddy said, "Now that wasn't so bad, was it?"

"It was for me!" replied Lily.

Sometimes what hurts for one person doesn't hurt for another. Everyone has different levels of how much pain they think is bad. Lily's daddy thought having stitches taken out didn't hurt, but Lily thought it hurt.

Jesus has His reasons for making you the way He did. Some people can deal with a lot of pain, and others can't. Whether you feel pain easily or not, it's part of Jesus' plan for you.

Your Turn

1. What was Lily scared of?
2. Did Daddy say having stitches taken out wouldn't hurt?
3. Did having stitches taken out hurt Lily?

Prayer

Jesus, thank You for making me the way I am. Amen.

Simple Ant Farm

Jesus made you unlike anyone else. You have your own unique way of feeling things and doing things. Isn't that great? Here's a special activity that's just for you.

What you need:

1. Dirt
2. Ants
3. Shovel
4. Water
5. Bread
6. Glass container (a jar or terrarium works well)
7. Fine mesh screen or cheesecloth
8. Cotton balls
9. Sugar

What to do:

1. With a shovel, scoop some dirt and ants into your glass container. Make sure you get your ants from the same colony, or else they will fight!
2. Place a cotton ball soaked in water and a small piece of bread soaked in sugar water into the container. These will provide enough food for the ants. You'll need to give them a new cotton ball and sugary bread every few days.
3. Secure the container's opening with the cheesecloth or screen.

Note: The ants will usually do some tunneling, but may start to die off after a week or so. Be aware that without a queen ant, the colony will be temporary anyway. Also, remember that some ants bite, so use caution when selecting yours.

God's Promise

We don't have to worry that another flood like Noah's will come.
Never again will I curse the ground.
~ Genesis 8:21

God's Promise

"I don't understand it," said Joy.

"What don't you understand?" asked Daddy.

"We learned the story of Noah at church. It said there was a flood that made water cover everything on earth, but how could that be? When it rains the water runs off the sidewalk and onto the dirt. It just gets soaked up. How could there be a flood on flat land?"

"After it rains for many days," explained Daddy, "the dirt can't hold any more water, so the flooding just gets deeper and deeper."

"That's scary," said Joy.

"Yes, it is," said Daddy. "But you don't have to worry because even though there are smaller floods, God gave His promise that He would never again send a flood like the one that happened to Noah."

Joy was right: it is scary to think of a flood like Noah's. You don't have to worry, though. God promised that He would never again send a flood to cover the whole world. And God always keeps His promises.

Your Turn

1. What did Joy have trouble understanding?
2. What did Joy think was scary?
3. Do you think another flood will cover the Earth someday?

Prayer

Jesus, thank You for Your promise to never again send a flood like Noah's. Thank You for loving us. Amen.

Your Own Flood

God promised that He would never again send a flood that would cover the whole world.

Joy didn't understand how the Flood could happen. After you complete this activity, you'll see how it all worked. Grab a pot or bowl and fill it with sand (you can use dirt or even just a large sponge, but sand is best). Take a full pitcher of water and slowly pour the water onto the sand. As the water begins to saturate and overflow the sand, talk about the Flood and how it happened in much the same way.

Doing Your Part

We need to finish when we make commitments.

For we are God's workmanship.

~ Ephesians 2:10

The Dirty Dish

"You still need to clean out the doggy's water dish," Mommy told Anna. It was Anna's job to take care of the dog each day, but she didn't like to clean his dishes. Even if the water dish was dirty, Anna would simply add a little more water.

"What's the difference?" whined Anna. "He still has water."

"You're wrong," said Mommy. "If the dish isn't clean, he could get sick."

Anna thought about her doggy and how sad she would be if he got sick. She didn't like to clean out the water bowl, but she didn't want her dog to feel bad either. It was her yucky job, but Anna finally decided that she needed to do it.

Do you ever fail to do part of a job? Anna gave her dog water each day, but didn't make sure his bowl was clean. Jesus wants you to always do your jobs the best you can. It's not enough to just do what you like to do; you have to follow through and do the *whole* job.

Your Turn

1. What did Anna dislike doing?
2. Why did Anna finally follow through and do her job right?
3. Is there some part of a job that you don't like to do?

_____

_____

_____

_____

Prayer

Jesus, please help me to always finish what I need to do. Amen.

Hard to Do

Sometimes it's hard to follow through and do what we're supposed to do. That's especially true when it comes to being a Christian. Look at the pictures below. Draw a line from the picture on the left that shows what you want to do, to the picture on the right that shows what you should do instead. The questions will help you to match up the pictures.

✳ What do you do instead of cleaning up your toys?
✳ What do you sometimes do instead of eating your veggies?
✳ What are you tempted to do instead of going to church?

Self-Control

Jesus wants you to be good even when you don't get what you want.

Jonah obeyed the word of the LORD and went to Nineveh.

~ Jonah 3:3

Faking Sick

Julia liked to be sick sometimes. When she was sick, Mommy would let her make a bed on the floor downstairs, watch television all day, and even eat in bed. Day after day she would ask Mommy to take her temperature to see if she had a fever. Mommy knew Julia wasn't really sick, so Mommy would lay her hand on Julia's forehead to see if she had a fever.

"You can't tell that way," insisted Julia one day when she really wanted to be sick. "You have to use the thermometer."

"No, I don't," answered Mommy. "I can tell when a child is sick just by touching them."

"That hand is bad," Julia yelled angrily. "That hand never says I'm sick!"

Julia thought Mommy's hand was bad just because it wasn't telling her what she wanted to hear. You shouldn't get angry just because things don't go the way you want them to. You should never scream at your Mommy, or say her hand is bad like Julia did. Jesus wants you to control your anger and be good, even when you don't get what you want.

Your Turn

1. Why did Julia like to be sick?
2. What did Julia say about her mommy's hand?
3. Can you remember a time when you lost control of your anger simply because you didn't get what you wanted?

_____

_____

_____

Prayer

Jesus, please help me to control my anger. Amen.

Slippery Goo

Jesus wants you to learn to control yourself. It's something you can do if you choose to and ask God for help. Something you can't control, however, is the slippery goo in this activity.

In a bowl, mix five tablespoons of cornstarch with three teaspoons of water and a few drops of green food coloring. Let the ingredients set for a few minutes. Once they've settled, try quickly sticking your finger in and out of the goo. See what happens? It doesn't stick to your finger! Next slowly insert your finger all the way into the goo and then pull it back out. What happened? This time the goo does stick to your finger, but the goo itself fills back in as if your finger was never there. Another fun experiment is to take some of the goo and roll it into a ball in your hand. As long as you keep rolling it, it will stay in the shape of a ball. If you stop, it will just go all runny and gooey again.

Doing My Best for God

Fairness

Jesus wants you to be fair in how you treat people.
Do not judge, or you too will be judged.
~ Matthew 7:1

Who Made the Snowman Melt?

"Turn it off!" Gabrielle yelled. The weatherman had just come on the television to give the weather report for the day. "Turn it off before Nicki sees it!"

"What's the matter?" Mommy asked, as she stood in front of the television so Gabrielle couldn't turn it off. "Why don't you want Nicki to see the TV?"

"Nicki hates the weatherman because she thinks he made her snowman melt," Gabrielle said.

Just then, Nicki ran out of the next room screaming, "No!" She ran straight toward the television set and hit the button to turn it off yelling, "Bad, bad!"

It's not fair to blame people for things that aren't their fault. Nicki thought the weatherman made the weather, but he just tells what it is. The weatherman doesn't make the weather. Nicki didn't understand that.

Jesus doesn't want you to blame people for things that aren't their fault. You have to be sure of what's happening before you make decisions about who did what. Jesus wants you to be fair in what you think and feel about people.

Your Turn

1. Why did Gabrielle want the television turned off?
2. What did Nicki think the weatherman did to her snowman?
3. Have you ever blamed someone for something and then later found out you were wrong?

Prayer
Jesus, please help me to be fair to others. Amen.

Weather Spinner

Jesus wants you to be fair in how you treat others. Nicki thought the weatherman made the weather what it was. It wasn't fair to the weatherman that she was mad at him.

Here's something you can make that the weather will control. If there's wind, it will spin around and around.

What you need:
1. Two paper plates
2. String
3. Crayons
4. Tape

What to do:
Color your paper plates with crayons. Now fold each paper plate into fourths, folding toward the outside of the plates. Connect the center edges of each plate together with tape. Tie string at the top and hang in a dry, windy location.

Overreacting

Don't overreact about things that aren't a big deal.

Direct my footsteps according to your word.

~ Psalm 119:133

The Worst Thing Ever?

Catrina had emptied the dishwasher all by herself. There had only been a few things in it, so it really hadn't been all that hard to do. She was very proud of herself.

When Mommy came into the room, Catrina showed her the empty dishwasher. Mommy praised Catrina for helping out, but told her that the dishes would all have to be put back because they were dirty. The dishwasher hadn't been run after they were put in it.

Catrina was so upset that she threw herself down onto the floor and howled, "This is the worst thing ever!"

"If that's the worst thing in life you ever have to deal with," said Mommy as she tried not to laugh, "then you're very fortunate."

Catrina had overreacted. Emptying the dishwasher while the dishes were still dirty wasn't that big of a deal. Mommy was still proud of her for trying to help, so Catrina should have been happy. Instead of being happy however, Catrina decided to act as if something terrible had happened.

If something's not bad, then you shouldn't act as if it is. Jesus doesn't want you to overreact to things or let little mistakes become big problems.

Your Turn

1. What did Catrina do to help out?
2. Why was Catrina so upset?
3. Can you think of a time when you got upset over something that really wasn't a big deal?

_____

_____

_____

Prayer

Jesus, please help me to not overreact to things. Amen.

Dirty Dishes

Jesus doesn't want you to overreact. If something isn't all that important, then don't act like it is.

Below is a picture of Catrina in her kitchen. Can you help her color the dishes that need to be put back in the dishwasher?

Good People

Being good isn't about being perfect.

Watch out that no one deceives you.

~ Matthew 24:4

Being a Good Person

Zoe felt terrible. She needed to have a grown up sign a form for her preschool teacher. Zoe forgot to have her mom sign the form, so she had her cousin sign it instead. When her teacher asked if her cousin was an adult, Zoe got scared and lied, saying that he was a lot older than her, even though he was Zoe's age.

Zoe told her mom what happened. She felt terrible that she had lied, and now it was too late to take it back. "I want to be a good person!" Zoe cried.

"It's OK," said Mommy. "We're all sinful, so everyone makes mistakes. The difference between being good or bad is what you do about your mistakes. If you learn from your mistake, and do what you can to make it better, then you are being good."

Zoe thought about that. Even though it was hard to do, Zoe told her teacher what she had done, and her teacher told her that it was mature of her to admit the truth. Zoe felt better and knew that Jesus would be proud of her attempt to be a good person.

Your Turn

1. Why did Zoe feel bad?
2. What did Zoe do to make the situation better?
3. How can you be a good person?

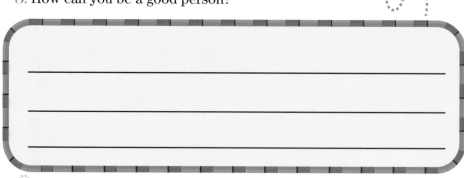

Prayer

Jesus, please help me to remember that being good isn't about being perfect. Amen.

Where's the Rolling Pin?

Jesus wants you to always try to be a good person, and doing that means following His word in the Bible. You can't hide bad things you do from Him.

Jesus wants you to be aware of things that are hiding! There's a rolling pin hiding somewhere in the room below. Can you find it?

Being Thoughtful

You need to be thoughtful of others.

Whatever you did for one of the least of these...you did for me.

~ Matthew 25:40

Not the Only Person in the Car

The car was full of children. Mommy was taking Andrea's sisters and some neighbor children to a movie. Everyone was talking at once, and Andrea's favorite music was playing on the radio.

As the car sped along, Andrea decided to sing. She sang loud and strong until everyone stopped talking...and started complaining instead. "Tell her to be quiet," yelled the other children. "We can't talk!"

"Andrea," Mommy said, "you need to stop singing. You're not the only person in the car."

"Why does that matter?" asked Andrea. "I just like to sing."

Mommy told Andrea that she couldn't always do whatever she wanted. Mommy explained that when other people are around, it's important to think of the needs of the others with you.

Jesus wants you to be thoughtful of other people. If what you want to do will bother other people, then you need to change that. Andrea liked to sing, and there's nothing wrong with that. She just needed to do it in a way that wouldn't bother others.

Your Turn

1. What did Andrea like to do?
2. Why did Andrea need to stop singing in the car?
3. Can you think of something that you chose not to do because you were being thoughtful of others?

Prayer

Jesus, please help me to be thoughtful of others. Amen.

Consideration Maze

Jesus wants you to be thoughtful or considerate of others, and not do things that will hurt or bother them.

Help Andrea find her way home. Pay attention to all the considerate things she could do in the car along the way.

All By Myself

Sometimes the best way to learn is to try something out.
Go and learn what this means.

~ Matthew 9:13

The Baking Baby

Baby Samantha wanted brownies and she wanted to make them herself. Samantha's big sister Claire, who was known as the "cook woman" in the family, didn't like that idea.

"I can make the brownies for you, Baby," offered Claire. "You can't do it by yourself."

"No," answered Samantha. "I want to make them!" She started to get the bowls and spoons out right away.

"Let her do it," Mommy said to Claire. "She needs to learn, and the best way for her to learn is for her to try it herself. You just watch to make sure she doesn't get hurt or make too big of a mistake. She can do it. She just needs a little help"

With a little help Baby Samantha did make the brownies. Claire had been afraid to let her sister bake by herself, but sometimes people learn best by doing. Since Jesus wants us to learn as much as we can, He would want you to do as much as you can by yourself, too.

Your Turn

1. What did Baby Samantha want to do?
2. Why did Claire think Samantha shouldn't make brownies?
3. Are there things that you learned by doing them all by yourself?

_____

_____

_____

Prayer

Jesus, please help me to learn as much as I can. Amen.

Artificial Ocean

Jesus wants you to learn to do as much as you can. The older you become, the better you will be able to take care of yourself—and other people, too!

Here's something you can do by yourself, but you'll need a little help from a grown up.

What you need:

1. Empty 2-liter plastic bottle
2. Water
3. Blue food coloring
4. Sand
5. Shells and artificial sea creatures

What to do:

This is a simple but fun activity. Just fill your bottle about ¼ full of sand. Now add your artificial creatures and shells.

Next, fill the bottle almost to the top with water. Put in a few drops of the food coloring to give it a blue tint.

Seal the bottle, shake it a bit, and lay the bottle on its side. When the contents settle, you'll have your artificial ocean.

Resurrection

Someday your body will die, but your soul never will.

I am the resurrection and the life.

~ John 11:25

The Wonderful Gift

Meagan and Joshua were friends. They had lots of fun together, but one day something bad happened—Joshua's daddy died suddenly. Meagan was very sad for her friend, and went with her Mommy to the funeral home where Joshua and his family had gathered to say goodbye to Joshua's daddy.

As Meagan walked up to the front of the room where everyone stood talking, she noticed the large box, called a casket. "Why is Joshua's daddy in there?" she asked.

"He's not really in there, honey," answered Mommy.

"What do you mean?" asked Meagan. She had overheard people saying he was there.

"When a person dies, his soul still lives. Joshua's daddy is in Heaven now," Mommy explained. "All that's in that big box is the body he used to live in while he was here with us. It's not really him."

Meagan thought about that for a long time. Meagan liked thinking that Joshua would see his daddy again when his soul went to Heaven too.

Jesus has given you a wonderful gift: eternal life! His death and resurrection have given you the promise that you also will rise to Heaven after you die here on earth. It's a wonderful gift.

Your Turn

1. Why did Meagan go to the funeral home?
2. What did Mommy explain to Meagan about the big box?
3. What will happen when you die?

_____

_____

_____

Prayer

Jesus, thank You for the gift of knowing my soul will go to Heaven someday to be with You. Amen.

Beautiful Butterflies

A butterfly is often used to symbolize the wonderful gift of Jesus' resurrection. A butterfly starts out as a caterpillar and then seems to be remade when it comes out of its cocoon as a butterfly. This reminds us of how Jesus was human just like you and me, and then rose from death.

Butterflies are such beautiful insects! They come in many colors and sizes. Wouldn't it be fun to make your own butterfly? Below is a butterfly that needs some color. You can make her look any way you like!

The Right Amount

**Jesus wants you to do things in the right amount
because it's healthy for you.**

But everything should be done in a fitting and orderly way.

~ 1 Corinthians 14:40

Computer Geek

"Computer Geek!" Faith yelled at her brother.

"Why did you call him that?" asked Mommy. "That's not nice."

"Well, he's on the computer, isn't he?" Faith responded.

Faith thought that her big brother was on the computer way too much. He was on it when she was sleeping. He was on it when she was playing. He was on it even during supper when Faith was eating. He was always on the computer!

"It's still not nice to call your brother a computer geek even though he's on the computer all the time," said Mommy.

"There's nothing wrong with me being on the computer all the time," Faith's brother chimed in.

"Yes, there is," said Faith. "Your brain is going to turn into mush."

While Faith was wrong to call her brother names, she was right that being on the computer all the time isn't a good thing. It's not healthy to do one thing all the time. If you have just the right amount of time, you don't do anything more or less than you should.

Your Turn

1. What did Faith call her big brother?
2. Why did Faith call her brother such a name?
3. Is there anything you do too much?

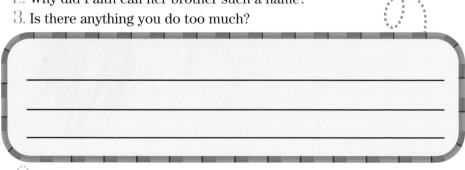

Prayer

Jesus, please help me to be healthy and do everything in moderation. Amen.

Note Holder

Jesus wants you to be healthy in every way. Doing things in the right amount is important for people of all ages—even your mommy or daddy can do too much of one thing.

One thing my kids can't get enough of, though, are these fun note holders. They like to hang them on their bedroom doorknobs so they can leave notes for each other.

What you need:

1. Paper plate (any type)
2. Construction paper
3. Yarn
4. Crayons or markers
5. Safety scissors
6. Glue or staples

What to do:

First, cut the construction paper into the same size and shape as one half of your paper plate. Decorate the construction paper and half of the plate with crayons or markers. Then, punch a hole on each side of the plate and thread yarn through to form a hanger.

Glue your piece of decorated construction paper to the bottom half of the plate. Staples actually work better, but if you're concerned about getting hurt with them, use glue. Remember: the construction paper should form a pocket; so only apply glue/staples along the curved portions when you are attaching it to the plate.

When the glue has dried, hang your note holder on your doorknob and wait for some notes to arrive.

Change

Only Jesus stays the same.
I the LORD do not change.

~ Malachi 3:6

Life is About Change

Kimberly was scared: so many things had been changing in her life. First, she and Mommy and Daddy moved to a different house and bought a new car. Then Mommy told her that she would soon be starting at a new school. Now the shed that once was little and safe was twice the size because Daddy added on to it. Everything seemed to be changing so fast. "I don't like it," said Kimberly. "Why does everything have to change all the time?"

"Life is change," said Mommy. "It's only natural that things change because every day we all get older and do new things. Nothing can stay the same."

"Nothing stays the same?" cried Kimberly.

"Well," answered Mommy, "nothing except Jesus. Jesus' love is the only thing you can count on to never change."

When Kimberly thought about Jesus, it made her feel good. Now she knew that no matter what happened, and no matter how many things changed, at least Jesus would always be the same for her—and He will be for you, too.

Your Turn

1. Why was Kimberly upset?
2. Why didn't Kimberly like change?
3. How do you feel about change?

Prayer

Jesus, thank You for never changing. Amen.

Changing Seeds

Everything around us will change. But not Jesus—He is always the same and we can always count on Him. Change can be scary sometimes, but it can also be a good thing. Knowing God is by your side can make change easier to face.

Below is an activity that takes some time to do, but can bring about a wonderful change.

What you need:

1. Seeds (corn or bean seeds work best)
2. Small planting pot
3. Dirt
4. Water

What to do:

Fill a pot with dirt and push your seed about an inch into the soil. Water and place in a sunny location. Turn your pot and sprinkle it with water every other day. Soon you'll see a beautiful green plant emerge from what was once a tiny seed.

*Note: this is a simple activity that shows how a seed can change into a plant. It's important to point out the beauty of the seed itself (texture, color and shape) before planting it to demonstrate that change isn't always from good to bad; it can be from good to good, too. Also, you might want to place a layer of clear plastic wrap over the top of the pot while the seed is germinating to help the soil retain moisture; remove the plastic wrap once the seed has sprouted.

Finding the Good

**With Jesus' help, you can be comfortable with
whatever happens in life.**
He will never let the righteous fall.

~ Psalm 55:22

Jesus Finds a Way

"Isn't that something," said the woman standing next to Carly. They were both looking at a dog walking by. Everything looked normal about the dog, except for one thing: he limped because he only had three legs.

"He lost his leg," said the woman, "but now he gets lots of extra attention. Isn't it amazing how he has learned to get around with just the three legs?"

Carly thought the lady was right. She remembered how Mommy had taught her that no matter what happens, you can always find both something good and something bad in it. Carly thought about the time when she lost her blankie for two days. It was awful, but it taught her that she could sleep without it. There were lots of times when something good had come out of something bad.

Just like with Carly, Jesus wants you to remember that no matter what happens in your life, you can find something good in it if you try.

Your Turn

1. What was different about the dog?
2. How did something good come out of Carly losing her blankie for two days?
3. Can you think of how something good came out of a bad thing that happened to you?

_____

_____

_____

Prayer

Jesus, please help me to find something good in everything that happens to me in life. Amen.

Aluminum Shapes

No matter what happens in your life, Jesus will help you deal with it and adapt.

Here's an activity that will help you be comfortable with change. You can make it work even if it's a little hard for you. Just keep trying, and you'll do just fine.

Ask your mommy or daddy for a few pieces of aluminum foil. The great thing about foil is that it will easily take any shape you form it into. Even wadding it up in your fist can create a shiny ball to play with. Try changing your pieces of foil into these shapes: a ball, a stick figure, a square, and a triangle.

My Way

What you want isn't the only thing that's important.

Humble yourselves, therefore, under God's mighty hand.

~ 1 Peter 5:6

My Song

Angelina loved her preschool class. They were always doing fun things. When the teacher told Angelina that she and the other kids should form a group and make up a song together, Angelina knew it would be great fun.

"I can sing my song for you," Angelina told Mommy when she got home. After she sang, Angelina told Mommy the song was just the way she had wanted it to be.

"Why is that?" asked Mommy. "Isn't the song a combination of what all the kids in the group wanted?"

"Everybody wanted to do it their own way," answered Angelina, "but I got my way because I was the loudest."

Jesus wants you to be clear about what you want, but He also wants you to help others have what they want, too. Angelina was only making sure that she got what she wanted. Angelina should have allowed the other kids to share their own ideas of the song and help make it up together. Then everyone could have felt good about the song.

Your Turn

1. What did Angelina and the other kids do in class?
2. Why was the song only the way Angelina wanted it to be?
3. Do you help other people get what they want, or do you only try to make things happen your way?

_____

_____

_____

Prayer

Jesus, please help me to think of others as well as myself. Amen.

Angelina's Way

Jesus wants you to help others get what they want sometimes.
Circle the picture below that shows what Jesus would want Angelina to do. Draw an X through the picture that shows what Jesus would not want Angelina to do.

Inner Beauty

How you look isn't as important as who you are inside.

The eyes of the arrogant man will be humbled.

~ Isaiah 2:11

The Slippery Snow Mountain

Mommy and Ella finished their shopping in town and started to walk toward the car. Ella was happy to be going home, but when she saw the giant pile of snow on the other side of the parking lot, she was even happier! The pile looked like so much fun that Ella couldn't resist running across to it. Mommy yelled to Ella that it was dirty snow that had been pushed aside by the snowplow, but Ella didn't care.

As she climbed to the top of the snowy mountain, Ella slipped. The fall caused Ella to scratch her cheek on the pavement. Soon a red, blotchy mark covered her little cheek.

When she got home, Ella showed Daddy her cheek, but he just laughed and said, "You'll live." But Ella was very upset.

Ella was so worried about how she looked that she started thinking her appearance was more important than anything else. Jesus wants you to remember that how you look is less important than lots of other things—like who you are inside.

Your Turn

1. How did Ella hurt herself?
2. What was Ella worried about?
3. Do you think how you look is more important than who you are inside?

Prayer

Jesus, please help me to remember what's really important in life. Amen.

Being Pretty

Jesus made you beautiful inside and out, but he wants you to care the most about who you are inside. That's where being pretty is the most important.

Here's a pretty activity for you to do today.

What you need:
1. White paper or colored construction paper
2. Safety scissors

What to do:
Draw a big circle on your piece of paper. You can trace around a bowl or other round object if it's hard to make the circle. Now cut out your circle and fold it in half. Then fold it in half again. Now fold it in half once more; it should be shaped like a small slice of pizza. Cut along the edges any way you like and then unfold. You'll find you have made a lovely doily that's like no other.

Talking About Jesus

You should tell others about Jesus whenever you can.

Go into all the world and preach the good news.

~ Mark 16:15

Sowing Seeds

Brianna was concerned about her friend Stephanie. Stephanie didn't seem to know about Jesus and never went to church. "I want to tell Stephanie about God," said Brianna one day, "but I don't know how."

"The best way is to tell her how you feel about Jesus," Mommy told her. "Don't tell Stephanie she's bad, or try to force her to listen to you. Just tell her what Jesus means to you."

Brianna thought about that for a long time. To her, Jesus was someone who loved her all the time and taught her how to live. However, when she told Stephanie this, Stephanie didn't really believe her.

"That's OK," said Mommy. "Maybe she doesn't understand right now, but what you told her may have sown the seeds for her belief later in life. Like a big plant that grows from a tiny seed, your few words to her now may grow into a strong faith when she's older."

Jesus tells us in the Bible that we should tell other people about Him. Even when people don't seem to listen, it's still a good thing to do.

Your Turn

1. Why was Brianna worried about her friend?
2. Did Stephanie believe in Jesus after Brianna told her about Him?
3. Why do you think some people don't believe in Jesus?

Prayer

Jesus, please help me to tell others about You. Amen.

Yeast Bag

Jesus wants you to tell others about Him. Even if they don't seem to care right away, your words may be like seeds—little thoughts about God that grow in their hearts over time.

Here's an activity where you sow another type of seed. Yeast is something that is used in a lot of your foods, including the bread you may eat at home. Yeast makes the bread rise (or get puffy) instead of laying flat. But did you know that yeast is a living thing? If you give it what it needs, it will actually grow. Do the activity below to see how it works.

What you need:

1. 1 package of dry yeast (or about 1½ tsp)
2. ¼ cup warm water
3. 1½ tsp sugar
4. Sealable baggie

What to do:

Mix the yeast and sugar together in the baggie. Add warm water and mix slightly. Seal the baggie and place it in a warm area (it doesn't have to be very warm; you just don't want it to sit somewhere cold).

Wait about five minutes, then take a look at your bag. You'll see that the yeast mixture is bubbling and the bag is expanding. That's because yeast is a single-celled fungi (type of plant) that needs to eat to grow. The sugar you put in the baggie is one of its favorite foods. As yeast grows, it makes carbon dioxide (a type of air or gas). That is what is filling the inside of the bag and causing it to get much bigger.

Wait 30 minutes or longer and look at your baggie again. What's it doing now? It's fun to see just how far it will expand.

The next time you eat a piece of bread, think about how the yeast in the bread made it grow, just like the air in the baggie.

Keep Trying

Keep trying, no matter how difficult something is.
Be strong and do not give up, for your work will be rewarded.
~ 2 Chronicles 15:7

I Can't Do It!

"I can't do it," said little Alisha for the third time. She was trying to scrub the floor where someone had spilled a cup of juice. It had left a spot that wouldn't come off, no matter how hard she rubbed.

"You'll have to just keep at it," answered Mommy. "It's your job to clean that part of the floor, so you'll just have to keep trying until you get it done right."

"But it's hard to do!" Alisha cried.

"Don't give up," Mommy replied. "Just because it's hard to do, doesn't mean you can't do it."

Alisha didn't want to keep trying. She wanted to give up. Cleaning the spot on the floor was hard to do. It would be so much easier to let someone help her. In the end, Alisha decided that she wouldn't give up—it was her job and she wanted to do it right.

Jesus would have been proud of Alisha. He wants you to do your jobs the best you can, and not give up just because something is hard.

Your Turn

1. What was Alisha's job?
2. Why did Alisha want to give up?
3. Can you think of a time when you wanted to give up?

Prayer

Jesus, please help me to keep trying, even when something is hard to do. Amen.

Alisha's Maze

Jesus doesn't want you to give up on something just because it's hard to do.
   In a similar way, the maze below is difficult to get through, but if you don't give up, you'll make it. Don't let yourself be guided down the wrong paths. Keep trying to finish the maze and reach the cross.

Being Ready

The Bible teaches me about God.

Our help is in the name of the LORD.

~ Psalm 124:8

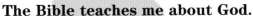

Goodbye Baby Bird

Jacqueline's friend Riley had come to spend the night. They played for hours, and then slept next to a clubhouse they built in Jacqueline's basement. It was a lot of fun, but the next morning was even better because they got to play with a baby bird they found outside.

Riley let the baby bird hop up and down on her robe and sit in her hands. The baby bird didn't fly, though. Jacqueline's mommy said it was because the baby was born with something wrong with it. She said it wouldn't live for very long.

Jacqueline's mommy was right. The next day the baby bird died. Riley and Jacqueline were sad, but they didn't cry. They knew it would happen so they had time to get used to the idea. Even though they didn't like it, they were ready for it to happen.

Sometimes even bad things don't seem so terrible if you know about them ahead of time. In the Bible, Jesus tells you that bad things will happen in life, but He will be there to help you. He lets you know that now, so that when something bad happens, you'll be ready to call on Him for help. He will make it easier.

Your Turn

1. Why did the baby bird die?
2. Were Jacqueline and Riley sad that the bird died?
3. Can you think of a time when knowing what would happen made things easier for you?

_____

_____

_____

Prayer

Jesus, thank You for being with me and preparing me to deal with things that happen in my life. Amen.

What's Different?

It can help to be prepared for what will happen in life, but regardless of what happens, Jesus will always be there for you.

If you like birds, then you'll be a little prepared for this activity. Take a look at the four birds below. Can you tell which beak is different?

Church

Like Jesus, a church should care about everyone.

I will build my church.

~ Matthew 16:18

A Healthy Church

The clipboard in the church library showed that only three people had checked books out in the last five months. "It seems a shame to keep this library open when so few people use it," said Mommy.

"If there wasn't a library, then where would those three people get their books?" Mason asked.

Even if it was just one person using the library, it seemed like it was worth it. Mommy had always told him that in a healthy church, every person mattered a whole lot, no matter what. Mason turned back to Mommy and reminded her of that.

"You're right," said Mommy. "This is a valuable library even if only three people use it. Thank you, Mason, for helping me remember that very important lesson."

Everyone matters to Jesus, regardless of who they are or what they're doing. He doesn't worry about time or money, but about caring for people.

Your Turn

1. What did Mommy say about the library?
2. Was the library worth keeping open for only three people?
3. Do you think there's ever a time when a person doesn't really matter to Jesus?

Prayer

Jesus, thank You for caring about every single person. Amen.

A Healthy Church

A healthy church cares most about people, just like Jesus.

Take a look at the pictures below. Circle the one that shows what a church should care about most.

Enjoyment

Jesus wants you to enjoy life.

I sing for joy at the works of your hands.

~ Psalm 92:4

Big Boots Night

It was Big Boots Night at church and Noah was so excited. All the children were supposed to wear the biggest boots they could find, and they loved it. Most had some type of extra large boots on their feet.

As Noah trudged into church, people took notice. He was wearing his daddy's big, brown boots, and he had to lift his legs high and hold his toes straight to keep the boots from falling off. The brown bootlaces trailed far behind Noah as he walked. He was quite a sight!

When all of the kids who wore big boots were asked to stand up in front, Noah was proud to say that his boots were his dad's. Everyone could see by the look on Noah's face that he was having a good time.

Jesus wants your life to be fun. He wants you to be happy with silly things, just like Noah. He even wants you to have a good time when you're in church. The life Jesus has given you is to be enjoyed.

Your Turn

1. What did Noah wear to church?
2. Why was Noah having fun?
3. What kinds of things do you enjoy in your life?

Prayer

Jesus, thank You for all the fun things You've given me to enjoy in my life. Amen.

Fun Boots

Jesus wants you to have fun. Below is a pair of extra big boots, kind of like Noah's. His boots were brown, but you can color these any way you want!

Friendship

Jesus wants you to be a friend to others.

*Greater love has no one than this, that he lay down
his life for his friends.*

~ John 15:13

Erin's True Friend

Erin was the new girl in the neighborhood. She didn't know anyone or have anyone to play with, so Leah decided she would help her.

Leah invited Erin over to her house. She played with Erin and introduced her to other friends. Leah made sure that Erin would never feel nervous or lonely and that she'd always have someone to be friends with.

One day, however, Erin started being mean to Leah. She said she had better friends now and didn't need Leah anymore.

Sometimes people seem to be something that they're not. Erin had just pretended to be Leah's friend because she was lonely. Once she had other friends, Erin forgot about Leah. Leah felt bad because she had trusted Erin, but Leah wasn't the one who was bad. Leah had done the right thing. Erin was the one who had done a bad thing.

Jesus wants you to try to be a friend to others whenever you can. Some people won't appreciate what you do for them, but that's OK. If you are a friend to others, as Jesus would be, then you're doing the right thing.

Your Turn

1. Why did Leah befriend Erin?
2. Why was Erin no longer Leah's friend?
3. Have you ever had a friend treat you like Erin treated Leah?

Prayer

Jesus, please help me to be a good friend to others. Amen.

Girl Friends

Jesus wants you to be a good friend to others.

Below is a picture of two girls who are great friends. Maybe you can finish coloring it with a friend.

Planning

You are always a star with Jesus.

Work...with all your heart.

~ Colossians 3:23

Being a Star with Jesus

"Let's start a band!" Shelby squealed with excitement. She had seen singers performing on TV and thought it looked like a lot of fun. Shelby imagined the kind of music her band would play and how lots of people would come to listen to them. Everyone would have such a good time—especially her.

"Why do you want to be a singer in a band?" asked Mommy.

"Because then I'll be singing on TV and everyone will scream and clap their hands for me. I'll be a star!" Shelby replied. "Call the TV man, Mommy, and tell him I'm ready!"

Shelby didn't realize that it takes a lot of work to be a singer and perform on TV. It takes practice and lots of time. You can't just call someone up and become a star.

Sometimes it's hard to get to do the things we most want to do. Shelby thought she could be a "star" right away. She didn't understand that it takes a lot of planning before that can happen. Shelby couldn't be a star on TV without many years of work and sacrifice, but she could be a "star" with Jesus, without doing anything at all.

Isn't it wonderful that as a child of Jesus, you don't have to do anything to impress Him? Jesus loves and cares for you. You don't have to plan or work at being a "star" with Jesus—He's already your biggest fan.

Your Turn

1. What did Shelby want to do?
2. Are you a "star" with Jesus?

_____

_____

_____

Prayer

Jesus, thank You for letting me always be a "star" with You. Amen.

The Stars in Your Life

You are always a "star" with Jesus. Below is a star that you can fill in with pictures of what's most important to you. We got you started by putting Jesus in the middle. Can you draw the other people and things that are important to you on the points of the star?

Stealing

Stealing is always wrong.
You shall not steal.
~ Exodus 20:15

All Stealing is Bad

"Why did you donate another book to the church?" asked little Jocelyn.

"Because someone stole the last one from the church library," answered Mommy.

"How could someone steal from the church?" wondered Jocelyn. "That's extra, extra bad!"

Mommy thought about that a moment. It did seem very bad to steal from church, but why was that worse than stealing from anyone or anywhere else? The Bible tells us, "You shall not steal." It's one of God's Commandments to all of us. It doesn't say that one type of stealing is worse or better than any other.

Stealing was still stealing, whether from a church or a candy store.

Jesus has taught us that stealing is wrong. Even though some stealing seems worse than others, all stealing is still bad. You should never steal from anyone, no matter who it is.

Your Turn

1. Why was Mommy donating another book to the church library?
2. What are some reasons why the book might have been stolen from the church?
3. Why is all stealing bad?

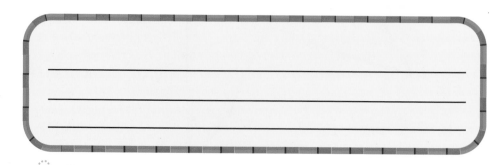

Prayer

Jesus, please help me to remember that all stealing is bad. Amen.

Mommy's Book

Stealing is bad, no mater who it's from or how it's done.

Below is a picture of Mommy's book that was stolen from church. Can you find a path through the maze and return the book to the church library?

Decisions

Trust Jesus to make the decisions for your life.

God is my salvation; I will trust and not be afraid.

~ Isaiah 12:2

Jesus' Plans for You

Standing before the class, the teacher told a story about her grandmother. She said that when Grandpa died, Grandma had her birth date put on the same grave marker. She had the words "Born 1913, Died 19—" on the gravestone. Grandma had decided that she would die sometime in the 1900's. The problem was that Grandma never imagined she would live as long as she did. She was still alive, and now it was past the year 2000! When she passed away, the date on her grave marker would have to be somehow erased and re-done.

We all like to think that the decisions we make are good ones. We make our decisions based on what we want to happen or what we assume will happen. However, what we want isn't always what Jesus wants to happen.

Jesus wants to help you to make decisions about your life. You need to remember that, no matter what decisions you make, only Jesus knows what's in store for you. When you trust Him, Jesus can help you make the best decisions for your life.

Your Turn

1. What did the teacher's grandma have put on her gravestone?
2. Why did the grandma do what she did?
3. Can you think of some decisions you've made that later turned out to be mistakes?

Prayer

Jesus, please help me to trust You to make the decisions that need to be made in my life. Amen.

Funnel Fun

Jesus knows what is best for you. You will make your own decisions, but always use Jesus as your guide.

This activity can be very fun if you make the right decisions, follow the instructions, and let your parents supervise.

What you need:

1. Small funnel
2. Black paper
3. Glue
4. Tape
5. Sand, sugar or salt
6. String
7. Tissue

What to do:

Tape a piece of string on opposite sides of the funnel. Tie the loose ends together and suspend the funnel above a table or over the floor.

Plug the funnel with a small piece of paper (make sure that you can easily pull it out the bottom when the time comes). Fill the funnel with sand, sugar, or salt.

Coat the dark paper with a thin layer of glue, and place it beneath the funnel.

Pull the plug out of the funnel and give the funnel a gentle push. The contents will flow out, forming an interesting pattern on the dark paper.

Experiment by pushing the funnel to obtain different results.

*Note: If you don't have a small funnel, you can make one out of a piece of construction paper and it will work just as well.

Bodies

You should use your body in Jesus' service.
Do you not know that your body is a temple of the Holy Spirit?
~ 1 Corinthians 6:19

Feet Are For Walking With God

The daycare teacher asked the children how different parts of their bodies were used. Spot by spot, each part of the body was pointed out. One by one, each child said what that body part did.

"My hands can carry things," said one little girl.

"My mouth is for talking," a boy called out.

When Hannah's turn came, she was asked what her feet could do. Hannah said, "My feet help me in my walk with God." The teacher paused for a moment, then said, "That's true, Hannah. Very good."

Jesus would have been proud of Hannah for her answer. Instead of just saying what each body part could do, she immediately thought of how Jesus used her body.

Your body isn't just made up of parts. Jesus gave you a body to use while you're here on earth. You live in it and it does certain things. What's more important, though, is how that body can be used for Jesus and what He wants you to do. Hannah understood that.

Your Turn

1. What did the teacher ask the children to do?
2. What did Hannah say her feet were for?
3. Can you think of a way your body helps you serve Jesus?

Prayer

Jesus, thank You for giving me a body to live in. Please help me to use it to do Your will. Amen.

Serving Jesus

You should use all that you have for Jesus.

Below is a picture of Hannah doing something in Jesus' service. She's helping her mother carry grocery bags into the house. In the empty frame, draw your own picture of something you do to serve Jesus.

Things We Don't Need

Jesus' love will never go away.

His love endures forever.

~ Psalm 118:3

What's a Rotary Phone?

"What's a rotary phone?" asked Mia one day, as she played with her toy phone. "I heard Jamie's mommy say they have one."

"A rotary phone is the old kind, before they had push-button phones," explained Mommy.

"How did they work?" asked Mia.

"Instead of buttons, the phone had a circle with holes in it. You just put your finger in one of the holes of the dial and turned it," said Mommy. Mommy went on to explain how the rotary phone worked, but no matter what Mommy said, Mia just couldn't understand. She wondered why people didn't use rotary phones anymore.

"We don't need them," said Mommy. "The push-button type works better now, so no one uses the other kind."

When Mia's mommy was little, the only type of phone around was the rotary phone, but Mia had never even seen one. As time goes by, there are things you won't need anymore, just like the rotary phone. Unlike other things in the world, however, Jesus' love for you will never go away. His love is as new today as it was yesterday, and He will always be the best thing for you.

Your Turn

1. What kind of phone did Mia ask about?
2. Why doesn't anyone use rotary phones anymore?
3. Can you think of something that you know people don't really use anymore?

_____

_____

_____

Prayer

Jesus, thank You for always loving me. I'm glad You'll never go away. Amen.

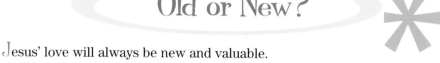

Old or New?

Jesus' love will always be new and valuable.

Below are some pictures of different objects; most of them are things that don't get used much anymore, but one is something that never gets old. Can you tell which is which? Circle the object that you think will never get old.

A Job to Do

Everything and everyone has a job to do.

There is a time for everything.

~ Ecclesiastes 3:1

Sick Chips

Amber was surprised when she saw the pile of wood chips on the floor at the store. She thought someone should clean them up.

"There's a pile of sick chips on the floor," she told her mommy.

"What are 'sick chips'?" Mommy asked.

"You know," said Amber. "When someone throws up on the floor, they put wood chips all over it so it covers up the mess. You know, sick chips."

"That's yucky," said Mommy, "but I can see why you came up with that name for it."

Everything has a job. Amber's "sick chips" were a type of wood chip. Their purpose was to soak up the mess when someone got sick. I'm sure you can think of lots of things that have a job to do, but what about you? Do you have a job?

The Bible says that Jesus has a job or purpose for each of us, including you! Even if you're not sure yet what your purpose is, Jesus knows. He loves you and will guide you to do His will.

Your Turn

1. What did Amber see on the floor?
2. Why did Amber call them "sick chips"?
3. Can you think of some things that might be part of your purpose?

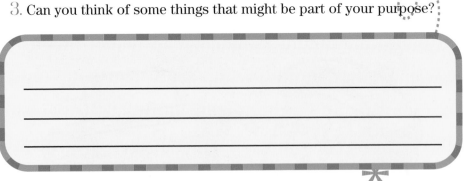

Prayer

Jesus, thank You for creating me for a purpose. Help me to follow Your will so I can do all that You want me to do. Amen.

What's My Job?

Everything has a job to do—even you!

Below are some pictures. Look carefully at each one and then tell someone about that item's job.

On My Own

Listen and learn so you can take care of yourself someday.

Watch and pray so that you will not fall into temptation.

~ Matthew 26:41

Listen and Learn

Melanie liked the commercial she saw on TV. It was a funny commercial about dentists following people around, catching them eating things that are bad for their teeth. She liked it, but she also thought it was a little scary.

"Is there really one of those guys who follows people around to see if they're having too much soda or candy?" Melanie asked.

"No, honey, it's just pretend for the toothpaste commercial," answered Melanie's mom.

"We don't need that because Jesus made us smart enough to be able to take care of ourselves," explained Mommy. "If you listen and learn what is good for you, someday you'll be able to make your own choices."

Melanie was glad that Jesus gave her the ability to learn and understand things. Jesus has made you able to care for yourself someday, too. If you learn from the Bible, and listen to your parents, you will grow into a person who can do lots of different things all on your own, just as Jesus has planned.

Your Turn

1. What was Melanie watching on TV?
2. Why do you think Melanie thought the commercial was scary?
3. Will you be able to take care of yourself someday?

Prayer

Jesus, thank You for making me grow so that I will be able to take care of myself someday. Amen.

Numbers Face

Jesus wants you to become self-reliant. He wants you to learn what you need to learn.

Take a look at the picture below. Can you pick out the numbers in the picture? It's OK to ask for a little help if you need it. When you're done, try making a few of your own pictures with numbers.

I Can Trust God

Wanting Good Things

You should never want to be like people who do bad things.
Do not let your heart envy sinners.

~ Proverbs 23:17

Only Want Good Things

"Look at those boys," said Audrey. She was sitting in the van with Mommy; they had just parked outside the pharmacy and could see two boys throwing rocks at the building across the street. The boys laughed as they threw the stones and then ran off. "Why can't I do that?" asked Audrey. "That looks like fun."

"You can't do that because it's naughty," said Mommy. "It's not nice to throw rocks at buildings because you could hurt someone or even break something."

Audrey wanted to be doing the same thing they were doing because it looked like they were having a good time.

As Audrey thought more about what Mommy said, however, she started to change her mind. The boys looked like they were having fun, but how much fun could it really be if what they were doing was bad?

Sometimes you might want to be like someone else and do what she does. Before you decide to be like that person, think carefully about what it is you really want. Jesus wants us to be like good people and do good things. He doesn't want us to imitate the bad behavior of others.

Your Turn

1. What did Audrey see some boys doing?
2. Why did Audrey want to be like those boys?
3. Do you ever want to be like people who do bad things?

Prayer

Jesus, please help me to want to be like people who do good things. Amen.

What's Good & Bad?

It honors Jesus when you choose to be like people who do good things instead of imitating bad behaviors.

Below are pictures of things that some people think are fun to do but are actually bad. There are also some pictures of people doing good things. Can you cross out the ones that are bad and draw a heart around the ones that are good?

Discipline

Discipline is good for you.

The Lord disciplines those He loves.

~ Hebrews 12:6

Time Outs are Good

"Can I come out?" shouted Jordan from the kitchen corner. She had been sent to the corner for hitting her brother. Jordan hadn't meant to hit him so hard. They were just playing, but Nathaniel said his arm hurt, so Mommy sent her to the corner.

"Why do I have to be punished?" Jordan asked Mommy when she was told she could finally leave the corner. "Why did I need a time out?" Jordan felt angry and upset.

Mommy explained that giving "time outs" was a way to discipline Jordan and Nathaniel when they did something naughty. "Discipline will help you and your brother grow up to live better lives," Mommy said. Jordan thought for a while and realized she understood what Mommy meant. She didn't like going to the corner, but it did help her remember to behave better.

Jesus tells us that discipline is a good thing. We know from the Bible that discipline is a loving thing as well. When your parents discipline you, it may not feel good, but try to remember that it really is for the best.

Your Turn

1. What did Jordan do to her brother that got her into trouble?
2. Why did Mommy send Jordan to the corner?
3. How does your Mommy discipline you?

_____

_____

_____

_____

Prayer

Jesus, thank You for my parents who discipline me. Even though I don't always like discipline, I know it's good for me. Amen.

Water Trick

Jesus would tell you that discipline is good for you. Discipline can teach you how to be patient so you can learn new things. Here's a new activity that I think you'll really enjoy.

What you need:

1. Drinking glass
2. Water
3. Cardboard
4. Bowl

What to do:

Fill the glass with water completely to the top, and then cover the opening with the piece of cardboard. Hold the cardboard firmly over the glass as you tip it over. Do all of this over a bowl—it will take a little practice before you can do it without spilling. Now remove your hand from beneath the cardboard. The water will be held in place by the cardboard.

The reason this works is because there is less water pressure inside the glass than air pressure on the outside. Isn't our world amazing?

Easter

The promise of Easter is that you are saved.

You were dead in your transgressions and sins.

~ Ephesians 2:1

Easter Sunday

Easter Sunday is so much fun, Michelle thought to herself. She was playing handbells in church with her brother and sisters. Michelle had practiced for weeks, and was so excited to finally be standing in front of the church with a bell in each hand. When the song started, however, Michelle's brother bumped into her, which made Michelle accidentally whack herself in the forehead with both of her bells. As the tears began to run down her face, she could hear Mommy next to her whispering, "Just keep playing, just keep playing." So Michelle did.

Michelle kept playing even though she was hurt. She knew that the purpose of Easter service was to praise Jesus. Jesus had suffered so much for Michelle that Michelle knew she could suffer a little for Him.

Easter is a time for thanking and celebrating Jesus for saving everyone from their sins. Jesus died on the cross and then rose from death on Easter. At Easter we celebrate God's promise that even though we sin sometimes, if we believe in Jesus, He will forgive all our sins.

Your Turn

1. Why was Michelle happy about going to church?
2. Why did Michelle keep playing even though she was crying?
3. Can you explain to someone why Easter is important to you?

Prayer

Jesus, thank You for the wonderful gift of Easter. Amen.

Gifts of Easter

Jesus gave you a wonderful gift on that first Easter Sunday. He gave you the promise of eternal life. Because of what Jesus did, you can go to Heaven someday.

Below are some of Michelle's favorite things about Easter. You can color each picture, and then draw your own favorite thing about Easter in the empty picture frame.

Creative Thinking

You need to find ways to do things, while still obeying God's laws.
Think about it! Consider it!
~ Judges 19:30

We're Still Touching the Van!

Emma and Jack rode with their Mom and Dad and were hurrying to help Aunt Sue with her dog.

Jack and Emma's cousins ran to the van to tell them what had happened. The children begged Mommy to let them get out. "OK," said Mommy, "but you have to always be touching the van."

Mommy went to check on the dog. As she disappeared around the back of the house, the children had an idea. They told their cousins to get a very long rope. Once they got the rope, Emma and Jack tied one end around the van door. Then they made their way along the rope's length, following their cousins around to the back of the house where they had seen Mommy go.

When Mommy saw the children, she gave them a stern look. Holding up the rope, they quickly explained, "We're still touching the van!"

Jack and Emma found a way to not disobey Mommy, while still getting to do what they wanted to do. That was very creative of them. They solved their problem and obeyed Mommy at the same time. I think Jesus would have liked that. He likes it when you find ways to get things done, while still obeying His laws.

Your Turn

1. Why did the children have to stay by the van?
2. How did the children find a way to get to the back of the house?
3. Can you remember a time when you were creative?

Prayer

Jesus, please help me to always use my mind to do Your will in the best ways that I can. Amen.

Swimming Raisins

Jesus wants you to use your mind to find the best ways to get things done while still obeying Him.

The best way to get this activity done is by following the directions below.

What you need:

1. A tall drinking glass
2. Water
3. 4 Tbsp vinegar
4. 4 Tbsp baking soda
5. 4 raisins

What to do:

Fill half the glass with water. Add the baking soda and then the vinegar. Drop the raisins into the glass. The raisins will "swim" because of the carbon dioxide created by the vinegar and baking soda. The bubbles will carry the raisins up and down!

Saying Sorry

You can't take away someone else's pain, you can only ease it.
Your consolation brought joy to my soul.
~ Psalm 94:19

Just Say You're Sorry

The four children gathered around the picture of a tiny kitten. Little Boots had been their cousins' pet, but he had just died because of an illness he had from birth. The children could see how sad their cousins were, and said things like, "It's OK, you can always get a new kitten," but it didn't seem to help.

When the children got home, Mommy explained why what they said didn't help. She said, "Pretend Vanessa just died (pointing at their ten-year-old sister). How would you feel if someone came up and told you it was OK because you could always adopt another big sister?"

"That would be terrible!" one of them cried. They understood that no one could replace Vanessa.

They understood what Mommy was trying to tell them. When someone is upset, the best thing to say is that you're sorry they are hurting. Jesus wants you to comfort others. No matter what you say, you can't take away another person's pain, but you can help to ease it by saying that you're sorry they're sad.

Your Turn

1. What happened to Little Boots, the kitten?
2. Why didn't the cousins feel better when they heard they could get another kitten?
3. What's the best thing you can say to help someone who is upset?

Prayer

Jesus, please show me how to help others in the best way I can. Amen.

Flowers

Jesus wants you to help others feel better. You may not be able to take away their pain, but you can comfort them and let them know they are not alone.

Flowers sometimes help people feel better. Here's a beautiful bouquet of flowers for you to color.

Creation

Only Jesus can create people.

Did not one God create us?

~ Malachi 2:10

The Body Shop

Mommy and Kaitlyn sat in the parking lot of the pizza restaurant, waiting for Kaitlyn's big brother to come out with the pizza they had ordered. As they waited, Kaitlyn noticed a car dealership across the street. A colorful sign hung on the building next to where the people sold cars, and Kaitlyn wanted to know what it said.

"The sign says 'Body Shop,'" answered Mommy.

"Why is that called the body shop?" asked Kaitlyn. That seemed like a funny name for a store. What could they do in a shop for bodies, she wondered.

"Is that where people get heads?" asked Kaitlyn.

Mommy laughed and explained that it was a place to fix cars. The sign said "body" because it meant the body of a car.

It was funny that Kaitlyn thought the car body shop was for human bodies. She thought that maybe they made parts for people there, but only Jesus can make people or their parts. Only Jesus can make you or me, or anyone else. We are all a part of His creation. He created the world and everything in it.

Your Turn

1. What was Kaitlyn doing when she saw the "body shop" sign?
2. What was the body shop really for?
3. Who makes people?

_____

_____

_____

_____

Prayer

Jesus, thank You for all Your creation, including all the people You make. I love You. Amen.

Hurricane Clouds

Jesus created all things on the earth, big and small. Only Jesus can make people. He is also the only one who can make a hurricane—but you can make something similar to a hurricane if you do this activity.

What you need:

1. Large mixing bowl
2. Spoon
3. Water
4. Blue food coloring

What to do:

Fill a large mixing bowl with water and stir around and around with a spoon until the water is spinning very fast. Remove the spoon. Quickly add several drops of food coloring to the center, and watch as the color moves from the center to the outside like swirling clouds.

Readiness

Jesus wants you to be ready for whatever may happen.

Always be prepared to give an answer.

~ 1 Peter 3:15

Be Ready for Everything

Avery was in trouble. She had been naughty and was worried that she might get a spanking. Avery thought and thought about what she could do to get ready just in case she was spanked, and an idea soon came to her.

Gathering up some training pants, underpants and sweatpants, Avery quickly began to pull them all on. After the first couple of pairs, it wasn't easy to get more on, but Avery tugged and wiggled, squirmed and squiggled her way into as many layers as she could.

When Mommy saw what Avery looked like, she couldn't help but giggle. Mommy told Avery that she would not have received a spanking anyway. A timeout in the corner was the best way to handle the problem.

Jesus wants you to be ready for whatever is going to happen in life. Sometimes you can't be ready, but many times you can. As it turned out, Avery didn't need to get ready for a spanking, but it was good to be ready just in case.

Your Turn

1. What was Avery afraid might happen?
2. How did she get ready for it?
3. Can you think of something you feared would happen and how you got ready for it?

Prayer

Jesus, help me to learn as much as I can about You so that I'll be prepared for whatever happens in my life. Amen.

Rainbow Planter

Jesus wants you to be prepared for whatever might happen in life.

Here's an activity that you can get ready for by gathering all the items you need from the list below.

What you need:

1. Cardboard milk carton
2. Tissue paper (in various colors)
3. Glue
4. Safety scissors

What to do:

Wash out the empty milk carton; measure about ¼ down from the top and then cut the top off. The size of the carton will determine the size your planter will be.

Cut your tissue paper into two to three inch squares. You'll need a lot of squares in order to cover the carton.

Next, make a little puddle of glue. Roll each of your tissue paper squares into a tight ball, dip in glue, and then apply to the milk container.

Cover the entire outside of the surface of the container and then let dry for 24 hours.

Now you're ready to add thedirt and plant a flower!

Joy

Jesus wants you to do things with joy.
For God loves a cheerful giver.
~ 2 Corinthians 9:7

A Cheerful Player

"I love the way Jonathan kicks the soccer ball," Aunt Lynn told her sister, Jonathan's mommy. "He kicks it with such joy."

All week, Aunt Lynn had taken Jonathan to his soccer practice, and all week she had watched him as he ran, kicked, and practiced with the other kids in the group. No other child would kick the ball into the air quite like Jonathan. Jonathan expressed so much joy in the simple act of kicking a ball that Aunt Lynn had to smile when she saw him.

What if, like Jonathan with his ball, you did everything with such a joyous attitude? What if, when you had to pick up your toys or clean your room, you did it with happiness in your heart? Maybe the job wouldn't seem like it was so bad.

The Bible tells us that God loves a cheerful giver. I'll bet that applies to most things in life. Jesus wants you to put all that you are into the things you do, and to do them with joy.

Your Turn

1. Why did Aunt Lynn smile whenever she saw Jonathan kick a soccer ball?
2. Why do you think Jonathan looked so happy when he kicked the soccer ball?
3. Do you do both fun things in life and your chores with happiness in your heart?

Prayer

Jesus, please help me to do everything with joy in my heart. Amen.

Secret Safe

Jesus wants you to do as much as you can in life with joy in your heart.

Having joy in your heart will be easy when you do this activity because it's a lot of fun.

What you need:

1. Empty paper towel tube
2. Clean glass olive jar
3. Elbow macaroni pasta

What to do:

Place the empty paper towel tube inside the jar and cut it to fit so that the lid can be easily placed on the top.

Then fill the area around the outside of the tube with the macaroni, leaving the center empty.

Now you can put the things you want to keep safe in the middle of the tube. The jar will look like it's simply full of macaroni, but it's really a safe place for all your important stuff.

Letting Go

Put your life in Jesus' hands.
Submit to the Father.
~ Hebrews 12:9

Flying Wheels

Seth was playing with his brother Caleb and cousin Sabrina in the driveway. It was a beautiful day and they were racing their toy trucks. Caleb and Sabrina would both send a truck rolling down the driveway and Seth would run with them to see which one went the farthest.

The next day, when Seth was telling his aunt about the game, he told her something interesting. "I saw Caleb move his truck with his foot when Sabrina wasn't looking so he would win," Seth said. "I told him I saw it, but Caleb just said he didn't do it."

"That's terrible," said Seth's aunt. "So what happened next?"

"Sabrina was mad," Seth explained, "but she decided to just go on with the game."

Sometimes it's hard to know if something bad has happened or not. Seth thought he saw Caleb cheat, but Caleb said he didn't. Sabrina didn't like losing, but she wasn't sure what to believe, so she decided to just keep playing. Life is like that, too. There will be times when you won't be able to find an answer or right a wrong. You will just need to put the problem in Jesus' hands and go on with your life. Jesus always knows the truth, so some things are better for Him to handle.

Your Turn

1. What did Seth see Caleb do?
2. Why did Sabrina keep playing?
3. Do you think you could keep playing if this happened to you?

Prayer
Jesus, please help me to put things in Your hands. Amen.

Measuring Tape

It's always best to put your worries in Jesus' hands and let Him help you to move forward. As your faith grows, it will be easier to trust Him.

Do you know what else grows with Jesus' help? Your body! Here's a way to watch your body grow.

What you need:

1. Construction paper
2. Tape
3. Safety scissors
4. Ruler
5. Unsharpened pencil
6. String
7. A clothespin

What to do:

Cut your construction paper into several long strips; make them as long as possible, but they shouldn't be more than two inches wide. You will need enough of these strips to make one giant paper measuring tape at least five feet in length. Just tape the pieces of paper together as you go.

Using a ruler, mark lines at one-inch intervals along the full length of your measuring tape.

Loop one end of the measuring tape around the pencil and secure with a piece of regular sticky tape.

Tie a string at each end of the pencil to form a hanger. Hang your paper measuring tape on a wall where you can easily stand against it to measure your height. Clip a clothespin onto the tape to mark your height.

If you don't want to leave the measuring tape out all the time, simply roll it up around the pencil when done and it will fit neatly into a drawer.

Take Charge

Jesus wants you to take control of things in your life.

The mind controlled by the Spirit is life.

~ Romans 8:6

Everyone Pile on Spencer!

The soccer coach's helper, Spencer, was yelling too much and everyone knew it. So when it came time for practice to end, the coach called the kids into a huddle and gave them one final instruction: tackle Spencer. Yelling and screaming as they ran toward him, they piled on top of Spencer, knocking him to the ground. Marisol thought she would love tackling Mr. Spencer, but she ended up on the bottom of the pile with the kids on top of her too!

Pushing and shoving, Marisol finally managed to make her way to the top of the pile, and then she had as much fun as the rest of the kids.

Sometimes you have to work at it a little if you want to make something fun. Jesus doesn't want you to just take what life gives you, He wants you to work at it a bit to make things turn out good. If you take control of what's happening, and just change a few things, you can often turn something that was bad into something good.

Your Turn

1. What did the coach tell everyone to do to his helper?
2. Why did Marisol have to change something before she could have fun?
3. Can you remember a time when you were able to change something that wasn't fun into something that was?

Prayer

Jesus, please help me to take control of things when I need to, so that I can make bad things good. Amen.

Name Squares Puzzle

Sometimes Jesus wants you to take control of a situation so you can make a bad thing good, or find a purpose for something that may seem useless. This is called taking initiative.

Here's a fun craft that turns something kind-of useless into something good and very useful. Get your parents to help you!

What you need:

1. Empty paper towel tube
2. Short, thin sticks
3. Hot glue gun
4. Two rubber bands
5. Thick piece of cardboard (the heaviest you have)

What to do:

Cut a round circle out of your cardboard so that the diameter extends just beyond the diameter of your toilet paper tube. Have an adult hot glue the circle to one end of your tube, making sure it is centered. Then, put your two rubber bands around the tube.

Now begin gluing the sticks to the outside of the tube. Thinner sticks work better, and don't worry about the length of the sticks—an uneven appearance just makes it look more natural. As you're applying your sticks, slip them

under the rubber bands, one by one. The bands help to hold the sticks in place while you're working and as they dry.

Once your sticks are glued in place and dry, remove the rubber bands. Now you have a fun holder for pencils, crayons, and even markers!

Being Smart

Being smart isn't always about being "right."

The intelligence of the intelligent will vanish.

~ Isaiah 29:14

Marked Trees

"What are those red marks on the trees for?" asked Isabella as they drove through the woods. She and her family were on their way to a place called Sleeping Bear Dunes, where there were giant piles of sand to climb, play in, and roll down. "Are those trees they're cutting down?" Isabella asked of the marked trees she was seeing.

Daddy was about to answer Isabella when her baby sister Kyra piped up. "No, that means they're maple trees," she said. She had seen Daddy mark trees in his own woods for when they would make maple syrup.

"That's a good guess," said Daddy, "but no, those trees are being cut down for road construction."

Baby Kyra's answer wasn't correct, but it was a smart one just the same. She had learned about maple trees and so Daddy was proud of her.

You don't always have to be right to be smart. No one person knows everything. What's important is that you try your best. Jesus wants you to always try to be smart and learn as much as you can. Doing your best is always the smart thing to do.

Your Turn

1. What did Isabella see as they were driving through the woods?
2. Did Baby Kyra answer Isabella's question correctly?
3. Do you always need to have the right answer to be smart?

_____

_____

_____

_____

Prayer

Jesus, please help me to remember that I'm still smart even if I'm not always right. Amen.

Personal Picture Frame

Even the smartest people are wrong sometimes. Jesus doesn't care if you don't have all the right answers, He just wants you to always do your best—that's the smart thing to do. In the same way, there's no single right way to do the activity below, but you will have to use some creative thinking to finish it.

What you need:

1. Small picture frame
2. Shells, stones, buttons, and other objects to put on the frame
3. Hot glue gun

What to do:

If you don't have an old picture frame around the house, check out your local dollar store or craft shop for an inexpensive plain frame.

Gather the materials you want to glue on your frame. Stones, shells, buttons, or even colorful pebbles and sticks gathered from the yard will work well. We have even used common driveway gravel!

Have an adult use the hot glue gun to fix your materials to the frame and let the frame set overnight. Once the glue is dry, put your favorite photo or a pretty drawing you've made into the new frame and enjoy.

Protection

You need to trust Jesus to watch over you.

You will protect me from trouble.

~ Psalm 32:7

Watch Over Me

"Remember to be good and not do anything you shouldn't," Mommy said as she drove Hope to church. It was children's field trip day at church and a whole busload of kids were going to an amusement park. Hope's mommy wouldn't be going along, but other adults (called chaperones) would be there to take care of the kids.

"I love you, sweetie," said Mommy as she hugged Hope goodbye. "Be extra careful and don't do anything that isn't safe." She knew Hope was a very good girl and very careful, but she still worried. It was hard for Mommy to put her little girl into someone else's care. She couldn't help but have tears in her eyes as she watched Hope walk away toward the bus.

It can be hard to give up our control and put ourselves, or those we love, in someone else's care. However, that's exactly what we do each day as Christians. We trust Jesus to watch over us just as Hope's mommy trusted the chaperones to watch over Hope on the field trip. Jesus is like your chaperone every moment of your life. He's always watching over you.

Your Turn

1. Where was Hope going?
2. Why was Mommy worried?
3. How is Jesus like your chaperone?

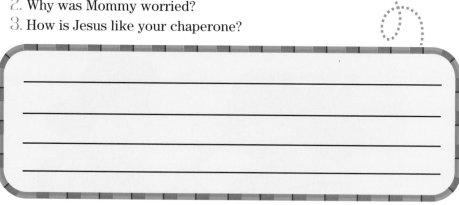

Prayer

Jesus, thank You for always being my chaperone. Amen.

Personalized Garden Rock

Jesus will always watch over you.

To help you make this personalized garden rock, you'll need someone to watch over you as well. A parent needs to help you with this project!

What you need:

1. Large, flat-topped rock
2. Hot glue gun
3. Small colorful pebbles

What to do:

The first step is to find a large rock that has at least one flat side. The side doesn't have to be completely flat, but the flatter the better.

Gather a variety of colored pebbles and have an adult hot glue them to the rock. It's best if you plan out your design ahead of time. Possible variations are to spell out a word with the pebbles, or to make a design covering the entire face of the rock.

Focus

Jesus wants you to focus on things that really matter.

What is highly valued among men is detestable in God's sight.

~ Luke 16:15

Keeping Focus

"Whoa, somebody ran out of their shoes," the coach yelled. It was the fourth day of soccer camp and the kids were having a great time. Every day, it was more fun to watch the kids than it was to watch the game itself. It was challenging as the kids learned the game. Through it all, the coach kept the kids excited and the game moving. It was all just part of the fun.

"Good job, Cody! Go with it," the coach yelled, encouraging the players when they needed it most. No matter what happened, he kept the play moving and shouted positive comments. The coach knew that having fun playing soccer was what was important, and he kept his focus on that no matter what else happened.

Sometimes it's hard to keep focus. The soccer coach remembered that fun is what counts when you're playing a game. In the same way, Jesus wants you to focus on things like love, family, and Him in the game of life.

Your Turn

1. Did the soccer coach focus on winning or having fun?
2. Why is having fun more important than winning?
3. What do you focus on in your life?

Prayer

Jesus, please help me to keep my focus on You and on what the Bible teaches me is most important in life. Amen.

Paper Bag People

Jesus wants you to remember what's important in life, and one of the things that's important is having fun.

If you do this activity, you're sure to have fun!

What you need:

1. Paper lunch bag
2. Crayons
3. Yarn, streamers, or baggie ties
4. Tape

What to do:

Decorate the paper lunch bag with crayons. The bottom of the bag should be the face of your person, with the edge showing the top part of the lips, and connecting to the bottom lips (as shown below). You can use the yarn, streamers, or baggie ties for hair. Yarn and streamers need to be taped on, but the wire ties can be poked through the paper bag.

Time

Jesus wants you to make time for the important things in life.

There is a time for everything.

~ Ecclesiastes 3:1

Making Time

"Come see, Mommy! Come see," yelled Destiny. Destiny was working on a new picture and she wanted Mommy to see it. Somehow it just wasn't as much fun unless Mommy saw it.

"I'm busy right now," answered Mommy. "Finish the picture first and then I'll come take a look at it."

"No, now," said Destiny. "It has to be now." As Destiny looked up into Mommy's eyes, Mommy could see the hope shining there.

"Well, OK," said Mommy. "I guess I can make time to see your picture now before it's done."

Destiny's face broke into one of the biggest smiles Mommy had ever seen. Mommy was glad she had made time for Destiny.

We all have stuff we need to do, but it's easy to forget that sometimes the most important things are the ones we don't have to do. To Destiny, having Mommy see her picture, even though it wasn't even done yet, was the most important thing in the world. Mommy didn't have to do it, but still it was a very important thing to do.

Your Turn

1. What was Destiny making?
2. Why was it important for Mommy to make time for Destiny?
3. Do you like your mommy to come see your projects? Why?

Prayer

Jesus, please help me to always make time for the truly important things. Amen.

Racing Balloons

Jesus wants you to spend your time wisely, and make time for the things that are truly important in life.

This activity is all about time—and speed! You'll need two people for this fun game, so grab a friend and get racing.

What you need:

1. 2 tube-shaped balloons
2. 2 pieces of string, each eight feet long
3. 2 drinking straws
4. Tape

What to do:

Thread each string through a separate drinking straw. Tie the first string to one end of the room and the other parallel beside it (at least two feet apart).

Blow up the two balloons, but don't tie them shut—just hold them closed with your fingers.

Tape one balloon to each straw (attach the balloons so that the untied ends are facing you). Now you're ready to race.

Hold the strings tight, then let the balloons go at the same time. Aren't they fast?!

Changed Plans

Jesus wants you to make adjustments to serve others.

Love your neighbor as yourself.

~ Matthew 19:19

Fussy Fishy

Mommy peeked around the corner into the classroom. Mommy had put Kristen in a children's summer class called "Science Exploration." They were learning lots of interesting things, but Kristen didn't seem to be doing anything except staring at something on the counter.

"Look, Mommy," said Kristen, pointing to a plastic bottle on the table. The top had been cut off and gravel and water added. "Look at the fishy."

"Whose is this?" Mommy asked.

"He's mine!" answered Kristen with a big smile. Mommy was glad Kristen was happy with her fish, but wasn't sure what to do with it to keep it safe. They still had a long time before they could go home and it was very hot outside. Mommy changed several of her plans for the day. It took a lot of extra time and effort, but it was worth it to see Kristen so happy.

Some things in life take a lot of changes to make them work out. Jesus wants you to make whatever changes you need in order to serve others.

Your Turn

1. What did Kristen get in her science class?
2. Why did Mommy have to make a lot of changes for Kristen?
3. What are some changes you make in your life?

_____

_____

_____

Prayer

Jesus, please help me to make changes in my life so that things work out right and I can serve others. Amen.

Soda Bottle Fish

Jesus wants you to make changes in your life.

Here's an activity that will require you to make changes to your life every day, as you will need to care for your fish.

What you need:

1. Plastic soda bottle (2-liter size)
2. Safety scissors
3. Colorful stones or marbles
4. Live fish/toy fish

What to do:

Cut the plastic bottle off about ¼ down from the top. Wash out the bottle, making sure you get all the soap out when you rinse it.

Fill the bottle with clean tap water. If you are going to put in a live fish, let the water sit for at least twenty-four hours. This helps to remove the chemicals that could be harmful to fish, and also brings it to room temperature.

Place a layer of colorful stones or marbles at the bottom of the bottle, and decorate with a plastic plant (or whatever you would like).

Now you can put your toy fish or small goldfish into its new home. Have fun!

*Note: If you use a live fish, change the water every couple of days and feed daily with goldfish flakes. Goldfish can grow quickly, and do better in a tank or larger bowl. This activity is only for short- term fun.

Creativity

Jesus gave you creativity to use.

His purpose was to create.

~ Ephesians 2:15

The Most Creative Hat

This Sunday was a special one: it was silly hat day. Tessa wasn't very excited, though, because she didn't have a hat. Everyone else had remembered to bring a hat to Sunday school for this special day—everyone except Tessa.

"What can I do?" wondered Tessa. Suddenly an idea came to her. Tessa had two shirts on, so she knew just what to do. Taking a book from the reading corner, Tessa carefully placed it on top of her head. Then she pulled the back of one of her shirts up over the top of the book on her head. It wasn't as pretty as the other hats Tessa saw, but at least it was a hat.

When the teacher saw what she had done, she pointed Tessa out as having the most creative hat. Tessa had gone from feeling terrible to wonderful in just a few minutes.

Jesus gave you creativity to use and it can serve you well. Just as with Tessa, if you use your creativity in a good way, you can make good things.

Your Turn

1. What special day was it in Sunday school?
2. How did Tessa make a hat?
3. Can you think of a time when you were creative?

Prayer

Jesus, please help me to use the creativity You've given me. Amen.

Creative Hat

Jesus wants you to use your creativity, and here's a great way to do it. Have your Mommy or Daddy help you out. Get a paper grocery bag, scissors, crayons, and some streamers or yarn. Take the paper bag and cut off the bottom. The hat should be big enough to fit over your head. Next, make an opening on one side for your face.

Decorate your "hat" any way you like. We like to use crayons on parts of it, and add multi-colored streamers to look like silly hair. You can also use yarn or even cotton balls to make it look like a silly wig.

Common Sense

Jesus wants you to use common sense.
No one stops to think.
~ Isaiah 44:19

Bowling Night

Bowling was one of Alana's favorite things to do. A couple times each winter, her family would meet her grandparents and cousins at the bowling lanes. They would bowl and eat pizza. It was great fun.

This time however, it wasn't so much fun. Alana didn't feel good. Her tummy hurt.

As the evening continued, Alana sat quietly holding a bag in her lap just in case she threw up, while the others bowled. A little later, Alana decided to loosen the belt of her pants just a bit—it was uncomfortable sitting down with the belt buckle pushing on her tummy. Not long after she loosened the belt, Alana realized she suddenly felt better. Could it have been that her belt was simply too tight? Soon she felt much better and was bowling along with everyone else.

Sometimes a problem isn't as big as it seems, and it just takes a little common sense to solve.

Jesus made you very smart, and sometimes all you have to do is think things through to find the answer to a problem.

Your Turn

1. Why did Alana stop bowling?
2. What caused Alana's tummy ache?
3. Can you remember a time when you found a simple answer to a problem you were having?

Prayer

Jesus, thank You for making me smart so I can find both simple and difficult answers to problems. Amen.

Bowling Night

Jesus wants you to use the brain he gave you and use common sense to find the answers to problems.

Here's a picture of Alana getting ready to bowl. She doesn't know which bowling ball to choose—can you help her?

Understanding

Jesus will help you to understand more things as you grow older.
When I became a man, I put childish ways behind me.

~ 1 Corinthians 13:11

The Monkey-Handled Toothbrush

"Are you still using the same toothbrush?" Mommy asked Brenna when she saw her squeeze some toothpaste onto her yellow, monkey-handled brush.

"I like my toothbrush," Brenna responded, giving Mommy a worried look. "I don't want to put him in the trash."

"Honey, it's time to use a new brush," Mommy said gently. "Your old one is really dirty."

"It's not dirty!" Brenna cried. "I wash it every time I use it."

"I know you do," said Mommy, "but some types of dirt can't be removed just by washing.

Brenna understood that Mommy was right, but it was hard to throw the old toothbrush away.

Is it sometimes hard to understand why you have to do certain things? Brenna couldn't understand the reasons for using a new toothbrush, but as she grows older Jesus will help it to make sense. Jesus will help you to understand lots of things as you grow older, too.

Your Turn

1. Why did Brenna need a new toothbrush?
2. Why did Brenna want to keep her old toothbrush?

Prayer

Jesus, thank You for helping me to understand more things as I grow older. I love You. Amen.

Toothbrush Art

Jesus will help you to understand more and more as you grow older. Brenna couldn't understand why she had to throw out her old toothbrush, but she will someday. In the meantime, she can use her old toothbrushes in a new and fun way. And so can you!

With an old toothbrush and a little paint you can make an outline of just about anything. For this activity, let's use a leaf. Just fasten the leaf down on a piece of paper. Dip your toothbrush into some paint (we water our paint down a bit so it's quite runny). Give the brush a little shake off to the side so you won't make any big globs of paint on your picture.

Now that your leaf is secured and your toothbrush is ready, start shaking the toothbrush around the edges of the leaf. You should have a fine but solid pattern of splotches outlining your picture. After the paint dries, remove the leaf and your work of art is complete.

Show Restraint

Jesus wants you to have control.

Have the wisdom to show restraint.

~ Proverbs 23:4

Cheese!

"Can I have some cheese?" Payton asked. She loved cheese; it was one of her favorite foods.

"Sure," said Mommy. "There's some in the refrigerator. Just take one or two slices, though."

Later that day when Mommy went to the refrigerator to get some cheese for the dinner she was making, she was surprised when she couldn't find the large block of Colby cheese that had been in there earlier. As she looked some more, Mommy noticed that the sliced cheese she thought Payton wanted was still there. "Payton," Mommy called, "didn't you eat any cheese earlier? I still see the cheese," Mommy said, showing it to Payton.

"Oh, not that cheese!" said Payton. "I ate the big round piece."

Payton had eaten the big block of Colby cheese, all by herself. That was a lot for one little girl! Payton did not show restraint when she went to have her cheese; instead of only taking a little bit, she had way more than was good for her.

Jesus wants you to use restraint when doing things. That means that He doesn't want you to just do whatever you feel like. You have to do what's smart—you have to think first.

Your Turn

1. Why did Payton eat the entire block of cheese?
2. Why was eating that much cheese all at once not good for her?
3. Can you remember a time when you didn't show restraint?

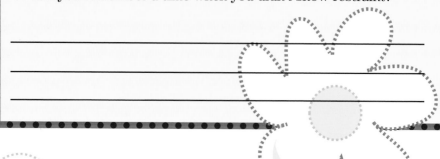

_____

_____

_____

Prayer

Jesus, please help me to remember that I need to show restraint. Amen.

Big Cheese

Jesus wants you to use restraint in what you do. He wants you to think about things before you act, and not just do whatever feels good at the moment.

Below is a picture of Payton eating a big block of cheese. Can you finish coloring the picture?

Secrets

Jesus doesn't keep secrets, and you can't keep secrets from Him.
God will judge men's secrets.
~ Romans 2:16

The Secret Closet

"I wanna go in!" hollered Veronica. Mommy had a special closet where she kept things she had purchased to give as presents and Mommy never let anyone else go in there. "Why can't I go in there?" Veronica wanted to know.

"You know that's a secret closet," Mommy told her.

"What's in there?" asked Veronica.

"Well, that's only for me to know," said Mommy. "That's why I call it my 'secret closet.'"

Veronica didn't like Mommy keeping secrets from her. She wanted to know what Mommy knew.

Not everybody keeps secrets, but some people do. It was OK for Veronica's mommy to keep her secret because it was a nice one, but that's not always the case. Not all secrets are good secrets.

One thing you can always count on is that Jesus will never keep secrets from you. You may not understand everything He does or says, but eventually you will. You can't keep secrets from Him, and He won't keep secrets from you. You can read lots of His answers in the Bible, and one day when you go to Heaven, He will explain anything else that you still do not understand.

Your Turn

1. What was in the secret closet?
2. Why wouldn't Veronica's mommy let her go in the secret closet?
3. Are there any secrets in your house?

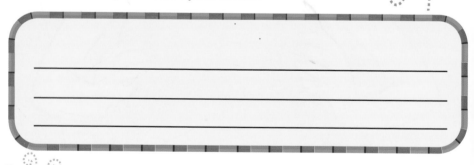

Prayer

Jesus, thank You for not keeping secrets from me. Amen.

Monster Marshmallows

You can't keep secrets from Jesus, and He doesn't keep secrets from you.

Here's an activity that isn't really a secret either, but not many people know how to do it. Ask your Mommy or Daddy for a few big marshmallows and a plate that can go in the microwave. Place your marshmallows on the plate and microwave them for about 30 seconds. Be careful: if you microwave for too long, they will burn.

As you watch, the marshmallows will grow bigger and bigger. They will get so big, in fact, that they will look like they're about to explode. When the microwave stops, you will notice that the marshmallows slowly shrink back down. It's great fun to watch and even more fun to eat. The marshmallows will be chewy and somewhat crunchy when you take them out of the microwave. Yummy! While you eat your marshmallows, connect the dots on the picture below and a secret word will appear.

*Note to parents: The marshmallows won't swell up just the one time—you can cook them for 20-30 seconds, let them shrink, and then do it again. It just depends on how crunchy you want them to be.

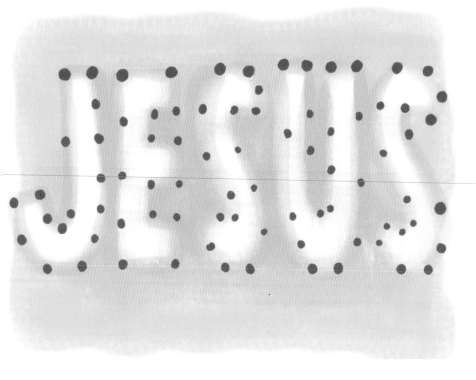

Work

Jesus wants you to work hard at whatever you do.

The worker deserves his wages.

~ 1 Timothy 5:18

Working with Uncle Kenny

It was a big day: Uncle Kenny was taking Caroline out to hoe the field with him. It was an important job to kill the weeds, and Caroline was going to get paid for helping. It was her first real job.

When she got ready for bed the night before Caroline prepared for her job by laying out her clothes and everything she would need. The next morning, Caroline got up early and ate a healthy breakfast. She packed a cooler of snacks and drinks because it would be a long, hot day. Mommy talked with Caroline about being serious and working hard (Caroline was sometimes quite silly), and she seemed to understand.

When Uncle Kenny finally arrived, it was clear that Caroline understood how important it was for her to be serious. Usually when Uncle Kenny came over, Caroline would snuggle and squeal with him, but this time she gathered up her things and went to get into the truck. She was ready to work.

Jesus wants you to work hard at your jobs. Caroline understood that she shouldn't fool around when she was being paid to work. She wanted to be a good worker and do a good job. Jesus would have been proud of her.

Your Turn

1. What was Caroline's first real job?
2. Was Caroline doing the right things to be a good worker?
3. Are you always a good worker?

Prayer

Jesus, please help me always to be a good worker. Amen.

Working the Field

Jesus wants you to be a good worker, just like Caroline. Below is a picture of Caroline in the field with her Uncle Kenny. Can you add to the picture by drawing in their vegetable crop?

Laziness

God doesn't want you to be lazy.
Whatever you do, work at it with all your heart.

~ Colossians 3:23

Too Many Pickle Jars

Daddy had been canning pickles, and Kendra was supposed to move two pickle jars down to the basement. Daddy told her that she needed to carry only one jar at a time and walk very slowly, so she could be certain not to drop any.

Kendra didn't want to carry the jars. She wanted to watch TV instead.

Instead of doing what Daddy had told her to do, Kendra decided that she would carry both jars at the same time. Then it would get done faster. Picking up the pickle jars, Kendra quickly walked to the basement. She wasn't careful. She didn't walk slowly. She didn't even pay much attention to what she was doing because she was thinking about cartoons instead. What do you think happened to the pickle jars?

Kendra dropped the pickle jars because she was being lazy. She didn't want to do the job the right way, or the careful way. She just wanted to finish quickly so she could go back to watching her cartoons on TV. The jars made a big mess for Daddy to clean up. There were pickles and brine everywhere.

Jesus wants you to be able to rest and relax, but He wants you to do things the right way, too. He doesn't want you to be lazy.

Your Turn

1. What was Kendra's job?
2. Why did Kendra do her job wrong?
3. Are you ever lazy?

Prayer

Jesus, please help me to do my jobs right and never be lazy. Amen.

How Many Pickles?

Jesus wants you to do your jobs well and never be lazy.

Here's something that might be hard to do, but don't be lazy! Keep at it, and you'll get the answer. Below are three of Kendra's pickle jars. Can you count the pickles in each one?

Volunteering

Volunteering honors Jesus.

A cheerful heart is good medicine.

~ Proverbs 17:22

The Big Health Fair

Each year, Mommy helped the church plan a big health fair. There was only one problem: Mommy always had a clown at the fair to hand out treats to the kids, but this year the lady who usually dressed up as the clown couldn't do it. It just wouldn't be as much fun without the clown.

"I'll be the clown!" squealed Allison, as she jumped up and down in excitement. Allison understood she wouldn't be able to spend the day playing and watching TV like she normally did, but Allison didn't mind volunteering her Saturday to help so many people!

The health fair turned out to be a big success. Allison's Aunt Sarah volunteered to be a clown too, and all the little kids were thrilled to see the clowns and get a special treat. It was a lot of work, just like Mommy had said, but seeing all the happy children made her work worthwhile.

I'm sure Jesus was proud of Allison for volunteering to help with the church health fair. He wants you to be willing to volunteer and help others whenever you can.

Your Turn

1. What was going to be missing at the fair?
2. Why do you think Allison volunteered to help?
3. Can you remember the last time that you volunteered to help with something?

_____

_____

_____

Prayer

Jesus, I want to help others whenever I can. Please help me to remember that volunteering is a good thing to do. Amen.

Clowns

Jesus wants you to volunteer whenever you can. Allison knew that and was wonderful in her volunteer job as a clown.

Below are three different clown faces and bodies. Trace them onto another piece of paper and color them any way you like. When you are done, have a grown-up cut them out. Then you can move the faces and bodies back and forth to mix and match.

Usefulness

God knew all about me when He created the earth.

But be glad and rejoice forever in what I will create.

~ Isaiah 65:18

Gathering Chestnuts

Kate and her sisters, Autumn and Melissa, were all sitting in the rain waiting for their brother to get out of school. Usually they had fun playing together while they waited, but today they were bored...until Autumn got an idea.

"There's a chestnut tree in the front of the school. Can we go pick up chestnuts?" Autumn asked Mommy, as the other girls chimed in. They loved to pick up the hard-shelled nuts. Chestnuts were so much fun to play with! Mommy agreed to drive them.

The girls squeaked and squealed in delight as they jumped out of the car and ran to the front of the school. They picked up so many chestnuts that their hands and pockets were overflowing.

It seems like a simple thing, but I think Jesus would have been happy to see Kate and her sisters using the chestnuts to play together. Jesus made a wonderful world for you to enjoy, and He doesn't want to see you waste it.

Your Turn

1. Why were Kate and her sisters waiting in the van?
2. What did the girls want to do while they waited for their brother?
3. Can you think of something that would get wasted unless you made good use of it?

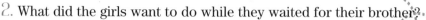

Prayer

Jesus, please help me to make good use of all the wonderful things You give me. Amen.

Good Uses

Jesus wants you to make good use of all the wonderful things He has given you. He doesn't want you to waste anything.

Here's an activity where you can find new uses for things. On the left side are two common items; another use for them is shown on the right. Think hard about a different way you can make use of a common item. On the left side, draw a picture of a common item, then on the right, draw another use for it.

Neatness

Jesus wants you to listen to your parents and be neat.
Children obey your parents in the Lord.

~ Ephesians 6:1

Neatness Counts

Dara and her sister Sophie wanted to play with modeling clay. They had a whole bag full of clay, with molds and other fun tools they could use with it. When they used the modeling clay, Dara and Sophie would spread an old tablecloth out on the floor, dump out the bag of molds and toys, and then create all kinds of wonderful things.

Mommy knew that Dara and Sophie always said they'd clean up, but they only did some of the cleaning. They still left a mess. The girls would get clay stuck on to their socks and carry it through the house. When Mommy reminded them of all this, the girls just answered, "We'll clean most of it up—we promise!"

"Well, that's not good enough today," responded Mommy. "I don't have time to make everything neat again after you're finished playing."

Your Turn

1. What did Dara and Sophie want to do?
2. Why did Mommy say they couldn't play with the clay?
3. Do you always clean up your messes completely?

Prayer

Jesus, please help me to pay attention to neatness. Amen.

Creative Crayons

Jesus wants you to pay attention to neatness and clean up any messes you make. This activity may cause a little mess, but I'm sure you'll clean it all up when you're done.

What you need:

1. Old, broken crayons
2. Old saucepan
3. Old cookie cutters
4. Wax paper
5. Empty soup can (optional)

What to do:

Remove the labels from your broken crayons and place them in an old saucepan that you don't care if you ruin. If you don't have an old saucepan, you can put the crayons in a clean, empty soup can, and place the can inside a saucepot surrounded by some water. Have your parents help with this project. Heat the crayons on "low" until they have melted, then pour the wax into your old cookie cutters—be sure you have the wax paper beneath the cookie cutters in case you spill. Let the wax set for at least 24 hours. Enjoy your new, creative crayons!

Being Protective

Jesus knows that sometimes it's good to be fierce.
The LORD your God fights for you.

~ Joshua 23:10

Protective Doggy

Bianca couldn't believe it. Her doggy Princess had always been such a sweet, quiet, gentle doggy.

One afternoon Daddy said that when he got home from work, he saw Princess corner a woodchuck that had gotten into their yard. It was snapping its sharp teeth at Princess. Princess barked and growled, and chased the woodchuck up onto a post at the far end of the yard. The woodchuck finally went away.

Daddy explained that Princess was protecting her territory. Princess was also protecting herself and her family from something that wasn't supposed to be there. Maybe Princess even understood that the woodchuck was mean and might hurt someone.

We usually think of Jesus as being very gentle, like how Bianca thought about Princess. We often think that He wants us to be gentle, too. However, Jesus was quite protective when He needed to be. When fighting evil or bad things, Jesus could be strong.

Your Turn

1. What did Daddy see Princess do?
2. Why did Princess fight off the woodchuck?
3. Are there times when you've needed to be fierce?

Prayer

Jesus, please help me to be fierce only when I need to be. Amen.

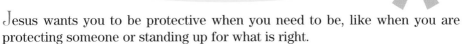

Gentle Princess

Jesus wants you to be protective when you need to be, like when you are protecting someone or standing up for what is right.

Here's a picture of Princess barking at the mean woodchuck. Can you finish coloring it?

Importance

Jesus wants you to know what the most important things are.

You have neglected the more important matters.

~ Matthew 23:23

Sleep or Talking?

Evelyn and Amelia loved their new bunk beds. They had waited a long time for bunk beds, and were excited to finally be sleeping in the same room. Evelyn and Amelia were only one year apart in age, so they had a lot of the same interests, liked the same books, and loved to play together.

The first night started out well. Evelyn was comfortable in the top bunk with her Teddy and books. Amelia was snuggled down below with blankie and her fluffy pillows. Everything was fine...for a while.

Each time Amelia was just about to fall asleep, Evelyn would once again start talking about something. Amelia told Evelyn to stop because they needed to get to sleep, but Evelyn wouldn't stop.

When Amelia complained that she couldn't sleep with Evelyn because Evelyn talked too much, Mommy explained about things that are the most important. Sleep is more important than talking when it's time for bed.

Jesus wants you to understand what's most important in your life so that you make sure these things get the attention they deserve.

Your Turn

1. What were Evelyn and Amelia so excited about?
2. Why couldn't Amelia get to sleep?
3. What are some things that are most important in your life?

_____

_____

_____

_____

Prayer

Jesus, please help me to remember what's most important. Amen.

Understanding Importance

Jesus wants you to understand and remember what is most important.

Below are several objects. Circle the ones that are most important to you, and draw an "X" over the ones that aren't.

Quick Behavior

Jesus wants you understand that impulsiveness can be bad.

If only they were wise.

~ Deuteronomy 32:29

Little Seeds, Big Surprises

Some time ago, Mommy had been about to pull a weed out of the flower bed when she realized it looked a lot like a little corn plant. Mommy decided to let it grow for a while and see what it really was. Now she knew it was a corn plant after all!

Before long, Mommy began to see corn plants in many other places around the yard. They were coming up all over.

After a while, Mommy learned the reason for the corn plants. Little Sierra admitted that when Daddy had planted the garden, she had taken some of the seeds and planted them all over the place. She hadn't really thought about what she was doing at the time, or why.

Sometimes you might do things quickly without thinking about why you're doing them—or what might happen because of what you do. Doing something without thinking can lead to bad things. Jesus wants you to think before you act. It's much better to think about what will happen before you do something.

Your Turn

1. What did Mommy find in the flowerbed?
2. Why were corn plants springing up all over?
3. Can you think of a time when you were impulsive?

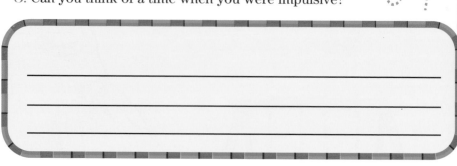

Prayer

Jesus, please help me to not be impulsive. Amen.

Impulsive Corn

Jesus doesn't want you to be impulsive. It's much better to think about what will happen before you choose to do something.

Below is a maze made out of corn plants. Can you help Sierra get to the farmhouse? Remember to think before you act.

Mix and Match

Jesus made us all with different likes and dislikes.
We have different gifts.

~ Romans 12:6

It's Great!

It was snack time and Lillian wanted to eat French fries, so Mommy made some for her.

Lillian went to the freezer and got out a tub of ice cream. Setting it on the kitchen table, she carefully scooped some out and placed it in a dish.

"What are you doing?" asked Mommy as she put a small plate of the fries in front of Lillian. "I thought you wanted some French fries."

"I do," said Lillian. She reached over to the plate, picked up a fry and dipped it into the ice cream. Then Lillian popped it into her mouth.

"Oh!" said Mommy with a grimace. "Does that taste good?" Mommy couldn't imagine that the combination of hot French fries and cold ice cream could taste good.

"It's great!" said Lillian with a smile, as she dipped her next French fry.

Isn't it wonderful that Jesus made us each different? I'll bet there are things that you like that are different from what other people like, too. There's nothing wrong with that. In fact, that's wonderful!

Your Turn

1. What did Lillian like to eat?
2. Why do you think Lillian liked to eat her fries that way?
3. What are some things you like to eat that are different from what most people like?

Prayer

Jesus, thank You for making me with likes and dislikes that are all my own. Amen.

Ice Cream Fries

Jesus made everyone different. We all have our own special likes and dislikes.
     Here's a picture of Lillian enjoying her French fries. Does that look good to
you? While you color the picture, think about some things you like that no one
else does.

Responsibility

Always fulfill your responsibilities.

Show this same diligence to the very end, in order to make your hope sure.

~ Hebrews 6:11

Cutie Cat

It was 1:30 in the morning on a warm day in July. It was very dark outside when Mommy heard a strange sound at the front door.

Carefully peeking through the window, Mommy discovered that Ariana's new kitten had gotten out of the barn, where it was supposed to be living.

"Wake up, Ariana," Mommy called. "You have to take care of your kitty. She got out."

Ariana opened her sleepy eyes and looked at Mommy in confusion. "It's the middle of the night, Mommy! I can't go out there," Ariana whined.

"Ariana," Mommy responded, "Cutie is your cat and your responsibility."

Ariana came down and headed outside to take care of Cutie.

Responsibility can be a hard thing to accept. Ariana loved the responsibility of taking care of her kitten when that meant feeding and playing with her. However, when she was responsible for taking Cutie back to the barn in the middle of the scary, dark night, caring for her kitten wasn't so easy to do.

Jesus wants you to take your responsibilities seriously, even the ones that are hard to do.

Your Turn

1. Why did Mommy need to wake Ariana up?
2. Why did Ariana want Mommy to take the cat back to the barn?
3. What are some of your responsibilities?

Prayer

Jesus, thank You for responsibilities and for the strength You give me to accept them. Amen.

Cute Cutie

Jesus gives us all responsibilities, and He wants us to fulfill them.
Here's a picture of Ariana's cat, Cutie, for you to color. Isn't she adorable?

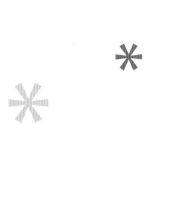

If You Liked **GOD AND ME!** You'll Love **GOD'S GIRLS!**

Hey, girls, get ready to add some sparkle to your look and a lot of fun to your life. *God's Girls* is packed with tips and ideas to help you make cool crafts. Plus you will read about Bible women and learn how to be a faithful Christian. There is even space included for you to write your deepest thoughts and dreams. So come on and join the party…you are one of *God's Girls!*

LP 48011 ISBN 10: 1-58411-020-1
ISBN 13: 978-1-58411-020-0

LP 48012 ISBN 10: 1-58411-021-X
ISBN 13: 978-1-58411-021-7

Bring God's Word to life with **THE GOD AND ME® BIBLE!**

God's mighty Word jumps off each colorful page of *The God and Me® Bible*. Bright illustrations, creative activities, puzzles, and games that accompany each Bible story will teach young girls ages 2-5 and 6-9 the wonders of God's power, truth and love for them in a new and fun way!

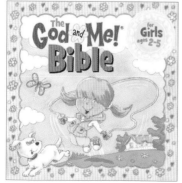

LP 48521 ISBN 10: 1-58411-088-0
ISBN 13: 978-1-58411-088-0

LP 48522 ISBN 10: 1-58411-089-9
ISBN 13: 978-1-58411-089-7

Journals Just for You!

Get serious about the Bible and have fun at the same time! These journals will inspire you to dig into the Word, while the stories and writing space will help you think, praise, pray, and grow. Choose from *My Bible Journal*, complete from Genesis-Revelation; *My Prayer Journal*, tips and hints for a better prayer life; *My Answer Journal*, real kids' questions about God; *My Wisdom Journal*, advice from Proverbs; or *My Praise Journal*, a celebration of Psalms.

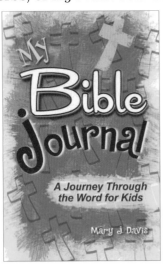

LP46911 ISBN 10: 1-885358-70-9
ISBN 13: 978-1-885358-70-7

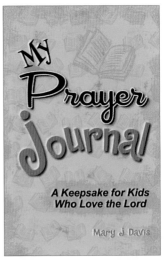

DB46731 ISBN 10: 1-885358-37-7
ISBN 13: 978-1-885358-37-0

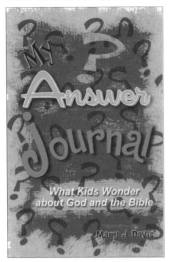

LP46931 ISBN 10: 1-885358-72-5
ISBN 13: 978-1-885358-72-1

LP46941 ISBN 10: 1-885358-73-3
ISBN 13: 978-1-885358-73-8

Devotions & More for Girls

Ages 2-5

God and Me 3

LEGACY PRESS®
www.LegacyPressKids.com